# PORTLAND

## YESTERDAY & TODAY ™

Ted Katauskas

WEST
SIDE
PUBLISHING

**Ted Katauskas** was educated in Chicago at Northwestern
University's Medill School of Journalism in the 1980s and was schooled in
New York City at The New Yorker's fact-checking department in the 1990s.
He has lived in Portland since 1998, where he writes for magazines, including
*Portland Monthly, Sunset, Travel + Leisure,* and *Food & Wine,* when he's not lost
in the archives of the Oregon Historical Society.

Facts verified by **Marty Strasen.**

Special thanks to Donald Nelson, Bruce Forester, and Troy Klebey
at Viewfinders, Thomas Robinson at Historic Photo Archive, the
Stanley Parr Archives at the City of Portland, the Oregon Historical Society,
and the University of Oregon Libraries, the Lake Oswego Public Library,
Edis Jurcys, and the Public Affairs Department at Reed College for
invaluable photo research and assistance.

Front cover: Downtown Portland
(Please note: The cover image of the city of Portland is a
composite image and is not to scale.)

Quote (page 40, "Pioneer Courthouse Square
is one of the first in a new generation of public squares...")
Copyright 2005, Project for Public Spaces, www.pps.org

In the early 1970s, Portland jackhammered a riverside highway called Harbor Drive and replaced it with the leafy, green Tom McCall Waterfront Park.

# Contents

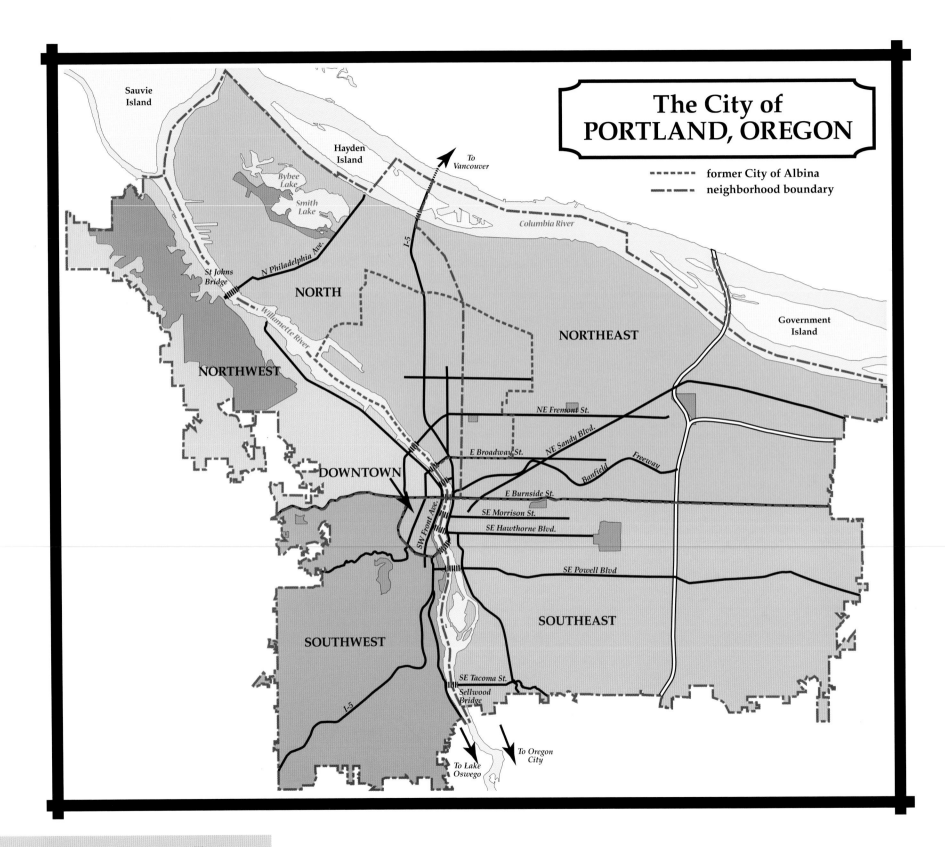

The City of
PORTLAND, OREGON

- - - - - former City of Albina
- · - · - neighborhood boundary

Sauvie
Island

Hayden
Island

To Vancouver

Bybee
Lake

Smith
Lake

Columbia River

St Johns
Bridge

N Philadelphia Ave.

NORTH

I-5

NORTHEAST

Government
Island

Willamette River

NORTHWEST

NE Fremont St.

E Broadway St.    NE Sandy Blvd.

Freeway

DOWNTOWN

Banfield

E Burnside St.

SE Morrison St.

SW Front Ave.

SE Hawthorne Blvd.

SE Powell Blvd

SOUTHEAST

SOUTHWEST

I-5

SE Tacoma St.

Sellwood
Bridge

To Oregon
City

To Lake
Oswego

# SPINSTER CITY

Portland has been appearing in newspapers and magazines as one of the nation's best places to live since 1885, when *Northwest Illustrated Monthly*, a national magazine based in Minneapolis, dispatched Thomas B. Merry to regale America with tales of his adventures in Oregon's outpost on the Willamette. Merry returned with *Portland: The Beautiful Metropolis of the Pacific Northwest*, a breathless travelogue spanning no fewer than 40 printed pages.

Merry seemed stunned, if not disappointed, to encounter not raucous buckskin-clad trappers but throngs of dignified gentlemen and corseted ladies. And instead of dreary log cabins and saloons in a primeval forest, Merry saw broad, tree-lined boulevards. Portland had an attractive, well-mannered populace living in a cosmopolitan city appointed with "countless evidences of New England civilization."

What made an even more indelible impression upon Merry was the undeniable evidence of Portland's prosperity, as told by the city's elegant mansions, which dominated the core of a thriving commercial district.

## MANSIONS FIT FOR A COW
Three decades later, in 1917, *Collier's Weekly* correspondent Wilbur Hall made a sojourn to Portland, and, like Merry, the Californian immediately fell under the spell of a metropolis wrapped in the embrace of the Willamette, flanked by the glaciated peaks of the mountains.

Also like Merry, what most impressed Hall were those outsized downtown mansions. But by 1917, the continously expanding city (population 204,592) had displaced all but a few. One of the most conspicuous was a three-story, Empire-style home with Corinthian columns, which was owned by the elderly widow of Oregon senator Henry Winslow Corbett, a respected Portland founder and financier. It wasn't the grandiosity of the mansion that captured Hall's imagination. It was the fact that the spinster Corbett had counterbalanced her home's pretension by pasturing a dairy cow on a plot of prime inner-city real estate, which was worth, by today's measure, more than a million dollars.

"I maintain here and now that I have found in this Corbett cow corral a concrete embodiment of the spirit of Miss Portland, spinster… she herself is just as she is," wrote Hall

And so Portland became known to Americans as the Spinster City, and the

This is a bird's-eye view of the Corbett mansion *(above, foreground)* taken from the cupola atop Pioneer Courthouse in 1878. The Corbett cow *(right)* is still grazing on the estate grounds in 1917.

Image cropped

The cityscape from this 1880s drawing looks as it did when *Northwest Illustrated Monthly* dispatched a correspondent to visit "The Beautiful Metropolis of the Pacific Northwest." After noticing the mansions that had been erected on generous plots in the center of town, the writer noted,

"In the city of Portland, notwithstanding the fact that it is barely forty-two years of age, reside twenty-one millionaires, and each has a residence set in the middle of a block. . . . In New York or Boston this same area of ground would be covered by the residences of some eighty families."

Corbett cow became as storied to Portlanders as O'Leary's cow was to Chicagoans. In 1952, Stewart Holbrook, a dashing Portland logger-turned-writer who cultivated a following as a chronicler of life in the romantic Pacific Northwest, lamented in his best seller, *Far Corner*, that the Corbett mansion had been torn down and replaced by a bus depot. He all but spat, "this is Progress." To Holbrook, Portland remained the Spinster City, cow or no cow.

## NO PLACE LIKE PORTLAND

By the 1950s, with the city population swollen to 373,000 due to wartime worker migration to the Kaiser shipyards, what defined Portland's ethos to Holbrook was that it thumbed its nose at skyline-defining office towers, unlike its more upwardly mobile neighbor to the north, Seattle.

"At about the same time the bronze plaque was being affixed, in order to call attention to the forty-two stories of a Seattle building, the Corbett cow grazing in downtown Portland was an indication that this overgrown village cared little whether or not it ever had a forty-two story building."

Portland finally received its 42-story building in 1984—a steel-and-glass office tower by Skidmore, Owings & Merrill, the firm that built Chicago's Hancock Center. Locals call it "Big Pink," for the way its rose-tinted windows glow when multiple ruby-hued shafts of reflected sunlight cleave the blanket of mist shrouding the slumbering Willamette. As striking as Big Pink may be, it doesn't define Portland: Monolithic towers aren't exactly embraced here, given

a 1970s-era city code limiting skyscrapers to no more than 560 feet. In certain respects, the municipal code that honors Portland's legacy as Spinster City is the one allowing every household within the city limits to keep a maximum of three hens. Recalling the Corbett cow, trios of contentedly clucking Wyandottes, Auracanas, and Rhode Island Reds now strut in the manicured backyards of stately Victorian, Foursquare, and Craftsmen homes in practically every neighborhood. Some urban farmers, in typical Portland anti-pretention one-upmanship, have augmented their flocks with herds of pygmy goats. Recently, a wayward four-legged lawnmower made national headlines when it wandered onto a TriMet bus. The incident didn't warrant so much as a brief in the city's paper of record. A goat riding public transportation—now *that's* the spirit of Portland.

As the ever-expanding city encroached upon residences, the Corbett home was torn down in 1936 and replaced with this bus depot, which writer Stewart H. Holbrook lamented as "blazing with neon, noisy as the sheet-iron roof of hell, and smelling twice as bad."

### U.S. Bancorp Tower

Portland's 42-story U.S. Bancorp Tower is known as "Big Pink" for the way its rose-hued face catches the early morning sun *(above)*. It dominates downtown Portland's skyline much like the distant peak of Mount Hood defines the eastern horizon *(left)*.

## Downtown

# BIRTH AND REBIRTH OF A CITY

Portland was founded on a cold, wet November day in 1843 when Asa Lovejoy, an agent of the Hudson's Bay Company, made an unanticipated detour. Lovejoy was ferrying William Overton, a sick and penniless Tennessee drifter, from a doctor's appointment at the company's Columbia River fortress near the mouth of the Willamette to his home in Oregon City, a settlement 26 miles upriver. Thirteen miles into their journey, Overton pointed out a 640-acre tract he had been meaning to claim for himself on the Willamette's western bank.

Francis Pettygrove          Asa Lovejoy

"He says to me, I am going away," Lovejoy recalled in an 1878 interview with a historian at his Oregon City farmhouse, four years before his death. "I have got enough of this country and if you want a claim, I will give you the best claim there is around here."

The Hudson's Bay agent ordered their four Native American guides, paddling against the swiftly churning current, to beach their waterlogged craft at a clearing. A footpath led into a dense stand of fir and hemlock that marched westward into forested hills a mile or so beyond.

"I got off and walked up the trail. It took my eye. I had no idea of laying out a town there, but when I saw this, I said, 'Very well, sir, I will take it.'"

Lovejoy agreed to advance Overton the 25-cent ($7.51 in 2008) filing fee in exchange for half of the claim's acreage, with Overton as the proprietor. Before he quit Oregon for Texas, Overton sold his share for $50 to Francis Pettygrove, an Oregon City shopkeeper and native of Portland, Maine, who had recently arrived with a boatload of merchandise from New York City. A few months later, Pettygrove and Lovejoy paid a carpenter to build a cabin in the clearing near the river's edge, at present day Washington Street, between 1st Avenue and Front Street.

"It was nothing but an old log house, and the mosquitoes were so thick that the fellow said he could not work," Lovejoy recollected.

In 1844, Portland founders Francis Pettygrove and Asa Lovejoy paid a carpenter to build a cabin in the clearing near the river's edge at present day Washington Street, between 1st Avenue and Front Street.

*Left:* By 1880, just 37 years after its founding, what formerly had been a thick stand of fir trees had been felled, and Portland, 17,577 strong, stretched from the waterfront to the West Hills.

## STUMPTOWN

The following spring, the founders hired a surveyor to carve the first 16 acres of their claim into 16 city blocks, each divided into eight 50×100-foot lots. Once they had mapped their townsite, they argued about what to call it. Lovejoy wanted Boston; Pettygrove, who had just opened a store near the cabin, insisted on Portland.

"We snapped up a copper," said Lovejoy, who decades later still seemed wistful about losing the penny toss. "I should

By 1916, Portland had grown into a modern city of more than 200,000—a hyperkinetic metropolis that would have been unrecognizable to the city's founders.

have named it Boston, because I am from there…but Portland is a very good name. From that it went on and did not amount to much for some time."

First, the forest yielded a few dozen cabins, followed by a blacksmith shop in 1846. In 1847, sea captain Nathaniel Crosby (great-grandfather of Bing) brought a prefabricated Colonial from Boston around the Horn and assembled it on the corner of 1st and Washington. By 1850, the year before Portland was incorporated, more than 800 settlers had arrived; so quick was the city's rise, stumps stood in the middle of Front Street and unsightly stubble dominated the landscape, earning the fledgling metropolis a nickname it's never been able to shed: Stumptown. By 1859, the last of the stumps on Front Street had been removed, and what once was impenetrable forest had been cleared all the way to the West Hills. Portland's 16 blocks had grown to more than 300, the number that approximates present-day downtown. All of the land had been taken and clear-cut, except for 22 blocks that girded the city's midsection like a green belt, thanks to the forward thinking of Daniel Lownsdale. Lownsdale was a tanner who had purchased Pettygrove's acreage (for $5,000 in leather) and had bequeathed the city its first public greenspace, the park blocks.

## THE DOWNTOWN PLAN

By 1900, downtown Portland would have been all but unrecognizable to Lovejoy. It was a cacophonous city of more than 90,000 people flitting about on streetcars and bicycles. And towering at the

heart of it all was the opulent Portland Hotel, an eight-story Queen Anne–style chateau that occupied an entire block at the city's very center and served as its social soul. In 1903, John Olmsted, nephew and adopted son of Central Park architect Frederick Law Olmsted, transformed a swamp north of the city into the Versailles-like grounds of the 1905 Lewis and Clark Centennial Exposition. The world's fair attracted 1.6 million visitors from afar who marveled at the almost-European city that had been carved out of the wilderness. In 1938, urban planner Lewis Mumford looked around and said, "You have an opportunity here to do a job of city planning like nowhere else in the world."

For decades, the opportunity went unrealized as Portland "modernized" its downtown in the manner of most American cities. Streetcar tracks were ripped up in favor of the automobile. In the 1940s, Harbor Drive, a freeway that separated the city from its river, displaced Front Street as downtown's waterfront thoroughfare. In 1951, the Portland Hotel was demolished to make room for a parking garage. By 1970, downtown had deteriorated into a crime-ridden ghost town at night and on weekends, as Portlanders scurried away in their cars to homes in the suburbs. Then, in 1972, Portlanders elected Neil Goldschmidt, who at age 32 was the nation's youngest big-city mayor. It was Goldschmidt's job to oversee an ambitious makeover—one designed to lure pedestrians back to the urban core—called the Downtown Plan. First to go was Harbor Drive in 1974; four years later it bloomed into Water-

Skyscrapers now define Portland's city center, but when Asa Lovejoy beached his canoe near this spot in 1843, an unbroken forest stretched from the Willamette's west bank to the hills more than a mile beyond.

front Park. In 1984, the parking garage atop the ruins of the Portland Hotel was demolished and replaced with one of the most famous public spaces in the world, Pioneer Courthouse Square. Two years later, the trolley bell was heard again as the Metropolitan Area Express (MAX), began disgorging hordes of passengers from the suburbs of Beaverton and Gresham into a transformed downtown.

While other city centers crumbled, Portland's downtown didn't just come back to life—it hummed. In 1992, architecture writer Philip Langdon, on assignment for *The Atlantic Monthly*, walked the streets and rode the MAX "to figure out how this courteous, well-kept city of 453,000, and especially its downtown, has become a paragon of healthy urban development at a time when most

American cities find themselves mired in seemingly intractable problems."

How indeed. Just as Lovejoy once wandered up a path and peered into an impenetrable thicket, Portlanders looked at their downtown ruins, embraced the challenge, and said, "I will take it."

# THE WATERFRONT

Since its founding, Portland has been inextricably tied to the Willamette River. When the city was young, the first, and for a long time the foremost, street was Front Street—an eight-block row of wooden two- and three-story storefronts built with their backs perched over the Willamette, offering easy access to cargo ships. Until the railroad arrived in 1883, the river was the city's highway; it was a link to the outside world, bringing clipper ships laden with sugar and pitch from Oahu and steam-powered paddlewheel boats from San Francisco with more and more settlers. Most importantly, it brought the mail, which attracted crowds to the main post office on Front Street with every landing.

As the city grew, it spread west from the waterfront to the hills. Successive fires in 1872 and 1873 reduced downtown to ashes, even burning the wharf down to pilings. But Portland rebuilt itself, its wooden storefronts giving way to cast iron and terra-cotta. And then came the deluges, first in 1876, again in 1880, then unforgettably in June 1894, when the Willamette, fed by a rapidly melting mountain snowpack, rose about 33 feet and overflowed its banks, submerging the Front Street business district and flooding downtown Portland west to 12th Street. An armada of 1,500 boats ferried shopkeepers and customers around downtown for three weeks. In the late 1920s, the city tamed its river by straitjacketing it in a concrete seawall. A six-lane highway, known as Harbor Drive, followed in the 1940s, cutting downtown off from its river for a quarter century. In 1974, Portland became the first city in America to remove an existing highway, jackhammering it to make room for Tom McCall Waterfront Park, reuniting city and river for good.

In 1847, Captain Nathaniel Crosby brought a prefabricated Cape Cod house from Massachusetts in his sailing ship, the *Toulon,* and assembled it on the southwest corner of Washington Street and 1st Avenue, one street removed from the nascent city's business district on Front Street. By 1859, three years after Crosby died during a voyage to the Orient, crowded by the city's ever-expanding commercial core, the home was relocated to 4th Avenue, between Yamhill and Taylor, by Crosby's widow. By 1904, when this picture was taken, what had once been the city's finest home had been converted to commercial use, housing a barber shop, plumber, and waffle shop.

In 1894, a cataclysmic flood inundated downtown Portland, an event chronicled with a commemorative souvenir pamphlet, "A Carnival of Waters," that celebrated the oarsmen who conducted "feminine Portland on sightseeing intent . . . They were ferried along the streets, and gay parasols and dainty garments flourished under the forbidding walls of grim wholesale houses along the water front almost as plentiful on Third Street, lately transformed into the Grand Canal."

### Front Street

In 1917, Front Street was clogged with freight wagons since the cobblestoned avenue was primarily a freight corridor; the city's commercial center had already migrated to higher ground several streets away from the river *(left)*. Front Street today *(below)* is known as Naito Parkway (in the background). The grassy knoll where businesses once backed up to the river (the seawall was added in the 1920s) became a highway called Harbor Drive in the 1940s and was remade as Tom McCall Waterfront Park in 1974.

# BRIDGES

Skyscrapers define most cityscapes, but Portland's landscape is defined by its bridges. For more than 40 years, Portland and its east side cousin, East Portland, were separated by an unbridged river that may as well have been an ocean. The event that marked Portland's ascendance into a city was the dedication of the wood-timbered Morrison Bridge on April 11, 1887. Built at the foot of Morrison Street by the Pacific Bridge Company, it cost $4.5 million at the present-day exchange rate.

The *Morning Oregonian* reported: "This new connection should be, and in our judgment will be, the beginning of very great things for both Portland and East Portland. It brings the two cities into closer relations and practically annihilates the physical barrier which separates them...We shall expect to see an immediate and rapid advance in population, not alone of East Portland but of Albina, Sellwood, Mount Tabor and throughout the wide stretch of country known as 'the east side.'"

The Steel Bridge—the first steel bridge on the West Coast—followed a year later, bringing transcontinental passenger trains trundling across the river and into the heart of the city. By 1891, as it annexed cities on the east side, Portland became the largest city in the Pacific Northwest; on the West Coast, it was only second to San Francisco, outpeopling Seattle until 1910. And as the city put down trolley tracks, it expanded in all directions. Six downtown bridges followed: the Burnside in 1894, the Hawthorne in 1910, the Broadway in 1913, the Ross Island in 1926, the Marquam in 1966, and finally, the Fremont, whose 310-ton, 902-foot-long, double-decker center span was floated on barges and jacked 17 stories into place in 1973. The first downtown bridge to be built in a generation—a proposed $254 million expanse designed to carry light rail trains and pedestrians from South Waterfront to the Oregon Museum of Science and Industry—promises to upstage them all. Sketches include a span with a windmill that generates electricity for streetlights and another with a mid-span park, but the most favored is an elegant, futuristic parabolic wave.

In 1910, workers rebuilding the Hawthorne Bridge (known then as the Madison Street Bridge) pause for a photo. The Hawthorne replaced two previous wooden iterations (one crumbled, the other burned) and has stood for more than a century; it is the nation's oldest vertical-lift drawbridge.

This 1894 cityscape shows the Madison Street Bridge (foreground, now the Hawthorne) and the Morrison Bridge. The Morrison was the first bridge over the Willamette and was made of timber at the time. The Burnside Bridge, under construction in the background, opened in July 1894.

In 1887, only one bridge spanned the Willamette. Today, downtown commuters have eight crossings to choose from (from the bottom): the Marquam, Hawthorne, Morrison, Burnside, Steel, Broadway, and Fremont bridges; the Ross Island (not pictured) is just upstream.

Pictured is a digital rendering of a proposed pedestrian/light rail bridge to span the Willamette between the Ross Island and Marquam bridges. If built, the futuristic wave-form design (a topsy-turvy mimic of the Ross Island Bridge in the background) will be Portland's ninth downtown bridge.

The New Market Theater is shown here in 1872, the year Captain Alexander Ankeny opened a 28-stall public market on the building's ground floor. Three years later, he opened an elegant 1,200-seat theater and café on the upper floors, where the Oregon Symphony debuted in 1882. The enterprise floundered five years later as the city's cultural and commercial center shifted away from the riverfront.

# PUBLIC MARKETS

When Captain Alexander Ankeny's 1,200-seat New Market Theater opened to a full house on the evening of March 24, 1875, with *Rip Van Winkle, The Daily Oregonian* reported that "under the glamour of a hundred gas jets, the theater presented a scene of dazzling brilliancy, the equal of which has never before been witnessed in this city." Being practical-minded, the captain anchored his second- and third-story theater with a public market on the ground floor; it was equally elegant with 28 marble-paneled stalls that became Portland's primary marketplace. But the city's cultural and commercial center shifted west with the opening of bigger and ever-more luxurious theaters, as well as the construction of the opulent Portland Hotel, and the curtain fell for a final time in 1887. The theater's market closed shortly afterward.

Nearly 50 years later, on December 14, 1933, more than 75,000 Portlanders came to see the new three-story Portland Public Market that opened just a few streets away. Spanning three blocks at the seawall, it was a cavernous building with stalls for 200 merchants, restaurants, a gas station, a beauty salon, a cooking school, and a three-acre rooftop parking garage for 650 cars. It also included a sugar mill touted as "a miracle of modern science where automatic scales controlled by photo-electric eyes weigh sugar to within 1-1000th of a pound accurately!" At the time, it was the largest public market located under one roof in America.

Like its predecessor, however, Portland's second public market soon fell out of favor and closed in 1942. The building was leased to the U.S. Navy as a warehouse during the war and then had a second life as headquarters of *The Oregon Journal* before it was demolished to make way for Waterfront Park. In 2009, Portland's Saturday Market—a funky outdoor art bazaar that's been held every weekend since 1974 beneath the Burnside Bridge just down the street from the New Market Theater—received a permanent home: an 8,000-foot canopy of steel, glass, and wood erected in Waterfront Park, just downriver from the old Public Market site. Meanwhile, a grassroots effort to resurrect the Public Market has been stalled since 2007, after attempts to site the project across from the New Market Theater, then at Union Station, went nowhere.

When the Portland Public Market (which also was called the Sea Wall Market because it backed the concrete sea wall) opened in 1933, it was the largest market under one roof in America. However, it only lasted for nine years.

**AMERICA'S CULINARY PATRON SAINT,** James Beard, who was raised in Portland, shopped at the Public Market before he relocated to New York City in 1937. He noted, "It was an education in food to know the public market as I did." Today, a grassroots movement called the Historic Portland Public Market Foundation wants to rebuild the market and name it after Beard.

A weekend craft bazaar known as Portland Saturday Market has operated in the square across the street from the New Market Theater since 1974.

A driver stops to water his team at Skidmore Fountain in 1888. Portland's first public artwork was meant to be functional: Four troughs for horses and metal cups dangling from chains could be filled from streams jetting from miniature lion heads.

# SKIDMORE FOUNTAIN

Stephen Skidmore was a wealthy druggist who traveled to Portland with his parents over the Oregon Trail from Illinois in 1850. When he died in 1883, he bequeathed $5,000 to the city for a public fountain that would be modeled after those he had admired at Versailles during a trip to the 1878 World's Fair. After raising an additional $18,000, the city's Fountain Committee, led by the lawyer and poet C.E.S. Wood, commissioned Olin Warner, a New York City sculptor who had trained at the Louvre and the Ecole des Beaux Arts. Warner's fountain was a 14-foot-tall masterpiece—a broad, shallow bronze bowl held aloft by two life-sized nymphs modeled after his wife. A veil of water cascaded into a granite catch basin and drained into four stone horse troughs, each with a metal cup attached to a chain that could be filled from spigots flowing from the mouths of miniature lion heads.

When Warner unveiled the fountain in New York in July 1888, New York City critics raved but also ranted. The *New York Tri-*

*bune* suggested Warner's fountain was too fine an achievement "for a western city with its bewhiskered, bepistoled lot of frontiersmen" and lamented that "it is unfortunate that a sculpture of this high quality could not be kept in New York."

The artist traveled to Portland and waited for two tense weeks while freight operators searched for the missing fountain, which had been inadvertently shunted to a siding in Walla Walla. In August, Warner assembled the fountain at the intersection of First, Ankeny, and Vine, at the very heart of old Portland, just across the street from the New Market Theater (which had closed a year earlier) and in sight of Skidmore's drugstore. For the dedication, brewer Henry Weinhard offered to prime the fountain with all the lager the city could drink, a feat that would have required a fire hose three-quarters of a mile long to connect the lager tun to the fountain nozzle, but city leaders soberly declined, opting instead to anoint the fountain with fresh spring water from the West Hills.

Skidmore Fountain and the New Market Theater
are shown in 1988.

New York City sculptor Olin Warner
used his wife as the model for the
twin bronze handmaidens that
support the bronze bowl of the
Skidmore Fountain, pictured here
after its 2005 restoration.

Fairgoers queue to purchase tickets outside of the main entrance gate at the Lewis and Clark Centennial Exposition during the summer of 1905. New York City landscape architect John Charles Olmsted took Guild's Lake, a mosquito-infested marsh on the outskirts of town, and transformed it into a gleaming city of whitewashed exhibition halls.

# LEWIS AND CLARK CENTENNIAL EXPOSITION

For four months in 1905, the City of Portland hosted the Lewis and Clark Centennial Exposition, a world's fair that drew 1.6 million visitors to fairgrounds that had been erected on a lake north of downtown. Although the fair was ostensibly billed as a celebration of the 100-year anniversary of Lewis and Clark's journey from Missouri to the mouth of the Columbia River, the exposition was Portland's first attempt to showcase itself to the world. And the world liked what it saw—so much so that many visitors elected to stay. In the five years following the fair, Portland's population swelled from 161,000 to 207,000. New York City landscape architect John Charles Olmsted, nephew and adopted son of Central Park designer Frederick Law Olmsted, transformed a swamp

on the edge of downtown into an ethereal city, with Versailles-like halls showcasing exhibits from 21 nations and 16 of the United States. The buildings, which weren't designed to outlast the fair, were constructed of plaster and wood, save one—the Forestry Building, a testament to Portland's prominence as the nation's leading producer of lumber. It was a 20,600-square-foot log cabin with a roof supported by massive pillars made of old-growth fir logs that were 6 feet in diameter and 50 feet high, each containing enough lumber to produce a 206×102-foot cottage.

Wrote one anonymous fairgoer from New York City in *The Independent:* "It was in this place . . . this spot where the strength of its ancient forests

and the vigor of its new-born cities have met in enduring hand-clasp, that Joaquin Miller stood on a Saturday in mid-July and received the many who came to greet him as poet of the Pacific and acknowledge that he had been a true seer when he wrote of their region years ago:

> Dared I but say a prophesy
> As sang the holy men of old,
> Of rock-built cities yet to be
> Along these shining shores of gold
> Crawling athirst into sea,
> What wondrous marvels might be told!
> Here learned and famous from afar
> To pay their noble court shall come,
> And shall not seek or see in vain,
> But look on all with wonder dumb!

On the morning of September 19, 1905, aviator Lincoln Beachey leaves the Lewis and Clark Centennial Exposition fairgrounds in the airship Gelatine, en route to Fort Vancouver, Washington.

This souvenir viewbook portrays the exposition's Government Building.

The Forestry Building was built with Paul Bunyan dimensions: The roof was supported by 52 old-growth logs, each 50 feet high and 6 feet thick. The building, which served as the city's Forestry Museum after the fair, burned to the ground in 1964.

# THE ROSE FESTIVAL

After its dizzying success with the Lewis and Clark Centennial Exposition, city leaders cast about for ways to sustain the excitement. Portland had become "The Rose City" in deference to the millions of buds that had been planted in parks and yards across town to beautify the city for its world's fair. Thus, in 1907, seizing on the newly adopted nickname, John Carroll, who relocated from Denver to publish the *Evening Telegram*, came up with the idea of an annual "rose carnival and fiesta."

A "Parade of the Roses," with flowers provided by local residents, was to be the main focus. Newspapers, including the *Evening Telegram*, put out requests the day before the first parade was to be staged, asking for as many flowers as the community could spare. People cut carnations, geraniums, roses, and poppies from their gardens all across the city and gave them to trolley conductors, who delivered the flowers to the parade's downtown staging ground, providing the 125 volunteer float builders with plenty to do.

On June 21, 1907, the evening edition of the *Daily Oregon Journal* gave a front-page recap of the successful parade. "Miles of rose-wreathed cars and cabs crawling at procession pace through the streets lined with thousands of celebrators; roses showered as greetings from friend to friend," it read. "The whole city, spurred on by the notable success of yesterday, has lent its aid in making complete in every detail the unprecedented display of floral beauty."

Over the ensuing decades, other events and pageantry were added to the celebration, including Rex Oregonus (a bearded king who arrived on a royal barge), a Rose Fleet (an armada of U.S. Navy ships), a Junior Parade and a nighttime Starlight Parade, a waterfront carnival, Indy races, and an air show. What was once a simple parade evolved into a party that lasted the whole summer. Although it has been scaled back in recent years, the Rose Festival remains one of the most popular civic celebrations in America, and the Grand Floral Parade continues as the main attraction, drawing 400,000 people to the curbs every June, second only to Pasadena's Rose Parade.

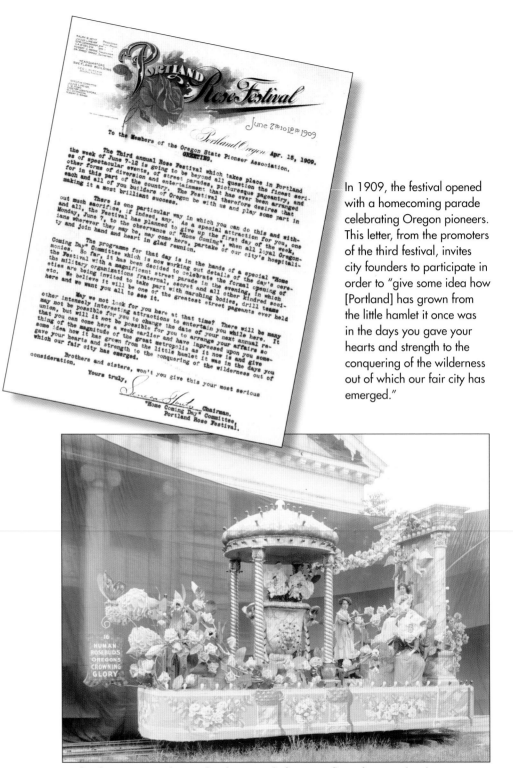

In 1909, the festival opened with a homecoming parade celebrating Oregon pioneers. This letter, from the promoters of the third festival, invites city founders to participate in order to "give some idea how [Portland] has grown from the little hamlet it once was in the days you gave your hearts and strength to the conquering of the wilderness out of which our fair city has emerged."

Portland's Rose Festival started with a parade featuring floats festooned with roses that were cut from gardens across the city. In this parade entry from the early 1900s, two children in a vase are masquerading as rosebuds.

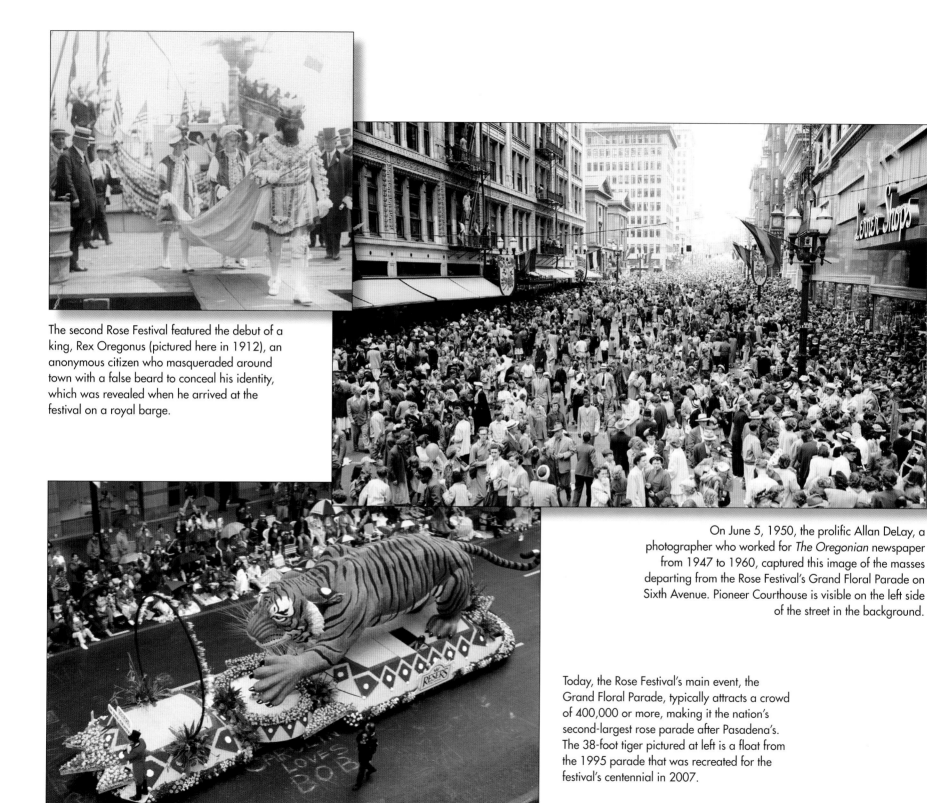

The second Rose Festival featured the debut of a king, Rex Oregonus (pictured here in 1912), an anonymous citizen who masqueraded around town with a false beard to conceal his identity, which was revealed when he arrived at the festival on a royal barge.

On June 5, 1950, the prolific Allan DeLay, a photographer who worked for *The Oregonian* newspaper from 1947 to 1960, captured this image of the masses departing from the Rose Festival's Grand Floral Parade on Sixth Avenue. Pioneer Courthouse is visible on the left side of the street in the background.

Today, the Rose Festival's main event, the Grand Floral Parade, typically attracts a crowd of 400,000 or more, making it the nation's second-largest rose parade after Pasadena's. The 38-foot tiger pictured at left is a float from the 1995 parade that was recreated for the festival's centennial in 2007.

# BENSON HOTEL

The Hotel Oregon (now known as the Benson Hotel), shown while it was under construction in 1912. Although advertised to open on January 1, 1913, its debut was timed to the inauguration of Woodrow Wilson in March of that year. Hundreds crowded the main entrance to be the first to sign the hotel's register.

The grand opening of the Hotel Oregon (as the Benson Hotel was first known) on March 4, 1913, was a theatrical affair, timed to coincide with the moment of Woodrow Wilson's inauguration. As hundreds of onlookers gathered on the sidewalk on Broadway, messengers from Western Union and the Postal Telegraph, two competing telegram companies, raced through the streets to be the first to deliver a dispatch conveying the news of the President being sworn in.

"The instant the message from the Postal Telegraph, which came a scant fraction of a minute in advance of the other, was received, Mr. Wright [the hotel manager] unlocked and threw open the doors and the crowd of people entered, each individual eager to achieve the honor of being the first to register," recounted the *Morning Oregonian*. "All through the afternoon and evening the lobby was filled with people who came to admire the new hotel. The lobby was bright with many floral pieces that had been sent . . . and upon a bulletin board were displayed a hundred or more telegrams of congratulations friends sent in from all parts of the United States."

After unlocking the doors, Wright telegrammed his congratulations to the President, informing him of the hotel's auspiciously timed opening—then went to the roof and dispatched two homing pigeons, each bearing a key to the hotel's front doors, to Simon Benson, a Portland lumber baron who had invested $1 million of his fortune in the hotel's construction before retiring to southern California.

Benson spared no expense on his hotel, which he modeled after the Blackstone in Chicago. He choose glazed terra-cotta for the building's exterior, a copper roof with French mansard dormers, and a 50-foot steel-and-glass marquee for its main entrance. The interior contained an Italian marble staircase and Austrian crystal chandeliers for its majestic lobby, which he paneled, as any lumber baron would, in exceptionally rare—and now extinct—polished Russian Circassian walnut felled from the czar's forest.

## SIMON BENSON

**BORN SIMON BERGERSON IN NORWAY IN 1852,** Simon Benson arrived in Portland 27 years later, penniless, to work in the forests felling trees, eventually earning enough as a logger to buy 160 acres of forestland on the outskirts of Portland. He formed his own company, which introduced a number of innovations to the industry. Most importantly, he introduced floating logs to California mills in massive ocean-going rafts that saved thousands of dollars per load in shipping fees. By the time he retired in 1912 at age 60, Benson had become one of Portland's wealthiest citizens and foremost philanthropists. Benson helped finance construction of the Columbia River Scenic Highway. He deeded 400 acres of land in the Columbia River Gorge— which included the spectacular Multnomah and Wahkeena waterfalls—to the city to serve as a public park.

Simon Benson also donated the prototype and first 20 models of the city's iconic "Benson Bubbler," four-bowl bronze drinking fountains, that were placed around the city.

*Above right:* The Benson Hotel soars above Broadway. *Right:* From its ornate coffered ceiling to columns paneled with walnut imported from Russia, the lobby of the Benson Hotel has changed little since it opened as the Hotel Oregon in 1913. The lobby was fully restored in 1990 to commemorate the 140th birthday of the hotel's founder—philanthropist and timber baron Simon Benson. Descendants of Benson and the hotel's architect, A. E. Doyle, attended the grand re-opening on September 9, 1991—declared Simon Benson Day.

# EQUITABLE BUILDING

The Equitable Building established Pietro Belluschi (pictured here in 1958) as one of the most influential architects of the 20th century.

When *The New Yorker* architecture critic Paul Goldberger came to Portland to lecture in late 2008, the only building he really wanted to see was the Equitable Building (which is also known as the Commonwealth Building). Aesthetics aside, it's arguably Portland's most architecturally significant structure, if only for its number of firsts. The Equitable Building was the first major skyscraper built in America after World War II, which accounts for another first: its aluminum skin. Portland architect Pietro Belluschi was a dashing young civil engineer from Italy who apprenticed with A. E. Doyle and who, at age 28, ascended to the firm's helm after Doyle's death in 1928. Belluschi, taking advantage of a surplus of materials left over from the manufacturing of military airplanes, eschewed conventional structural stone for the exterior of his commission and instead hung a "curtain" of aluminum and hermetically sealed double-paned glass. Another first: The Equitable was the first modern office tower built with windows that didn't open, and because of this, Belluschi developed a specialized climate control system that incorporated an innovation known as a heat pump to regulate the temperature and circulate air. When the 12-story building (later expanded to 13) was completed in 1948, no one had seen anything like it.

"Why, the first thing that came on the Equitable Building with all that glass, the new use of glass, all of the same size in double thickness for climate control, we found how the sky was reflecting," Belluschi recalled in a 1984 interview for the Smithsonian Institution's Northwest Oral History Project. "The clouds moving through the sky—you could see it, and the building looked like it was moving because the clouds were moving."

In breaking the mold in 1948 with the Equitable Building—the first office tower built in America after World War II—Portland architect Pietro Belluschi unleashed a wave of a copycat metal-and-glass-sheathed boxes that redefined cityscapes around the world. The classical, columned building just across the street from the Equitable, the U.S. National Bank Building, was designed by Belluschi's mentor, A. E. Doyle, in 1916.

### The Building of Firsts

The Equitable Building was the world's first hermetically sealed skyscraper, designed with windows that couldn't be opened. Aside from letting in copious amounts of natural daylight, the glass curtain transformed Belluschi's skyscraper into a sky reflector.

Just as Mount Hood stands out from the many lesser peaks of the Cascade range, Pietro Belluschi's rose-hued bank tower (left, middle ground) distinguishes itself from the many lowrise office towers of downtown Portland.

# U.S. BANCORP TOWER

A. E. Doyle—the architect who designed many of Portland's significant buildings in the early 20th century—often said that the area around the old New Market Theater needed a skyline-defining bank tower. In 1983, more than half a century after his death, Doyle's wish was realized with the U.S. Bancorp Tower, which Skidmore Owings & Merrill (the Chicago-based firm noted for New York City's Freedom Tower and the Burj Dubai) designed in consultation with Doyle's celebrated protégé, Pietro Belluschi. At 536 feet, the 42-story glass and

granite tower isn't Portland's tallest skyscraper, but it's often described as the city's most striking due to the way that its hue and mirrored windows change color as the sun tracks across the sky, giving rise to the tower's local nickname, "Big Pink." The building boasts 1.1 million square feet of office space and an unparalleled view: With a 360-degree panorama of the Cascade and Coast mountain ranges, Big Pink's 30th-floor dining room and lounge, the Portland City Grill, is the city's highest and most profitable restaurant.

## Big Pink

The U.S. Bancorp Tower, completed in 1983, is Portland's second-tallest skyscraper. The first is Portland's other bank tower, the Wells Fargo Center, which was built a decade earlier and bests Pietro Belluschi's tower by a scant eight feet. The Bancorp Tower earned its nickname, "Big Pink," for the way its rose-hued windows and granite façade glow in the ever-changing light of Portland's sun, which is often AWOL.

# THE PORTLAND BUILDING

Although the Equitable Building may be the city's signature groundbreaking work of architecture, Michael Graves's Portland Building certainly could be deemed the most controversial. Built to house the city's civil servants under a single roof, its most vociferous critic was none other than Pietro Belluschi. He appeared before the city council in 1979 in an attempt to derail the commission, arguing that Graves's "oversized beribboned Christmas package" was more appropriate for Las Vegas than Portland. Perhaps he was smarting from the fact that the city's design review board—which chose Graves's design over ten others—had hired Belluschi's nemesis, New York City-based Philip Johnson, as its architectural advisor instead of its hometown hero. Regardless, the mayor greenlighted Graves's upside-down cake of a Portland Building because "the Graves plan offered prospects of national architectural recognition," which it received and then some—the building's unveiling in 1982 promptly ignited a firestorm of debate, splashed on the cover of both *Newsweek* and *TIME* as an example of postmodernism excess. "The Portland building is dangerous," admonished *TIME*'s architecture critic, Wolf Von Eckardt. "Modern architecture is ripe for a radical change, but Graves would replace Satan with Beelzebub."

Understanding what it's like to be demonized for breaking the mold, Belluschi later tempered his criticism, saying, "You don't admire the thunder for having broken the tree, but somehow it wakes everybody up and puts you on the alert and makes [you] aware that there is another point of view, even if you disagree violently with it."

The 36-foot-tall *Portlandia* statue by Washington, D.C., sculptor Raymond Kaskey was shipped to Portland in pieces by train in October 1985, reassembled at a barge-building facility, then traveled up the Willamette River on a barge.

Once *Portlandia* reached downtown Portland, a truck transported the 6.5-ton statue to the Portland Building, where a crane hoisted it to its perch above the building's main entrance. Inspired by the Lady of Commerce depicted on the 1851 seal of the city, *Portlandia* is the second-largest hammered copper sculpture in the country, after the Statue of Liberty.

When it was dedicated in 1982, Michael Graves's Portland Building ignited a firestorm of controversy about the excesses of postmodernist design. "The controversy over whether it is 'three dimensional poetry,' an 'adventurous,' 'innovative,' 'exciting' piece of architecture or a 'jukebox,' 'Christmas package,' or 'turkey' may never end," sums up the city's official Portland Building pamphlet. "One thing is certain: it has drawn national attention to Portland."

# CITY HALL

Initial designs for Portland's first city hall called for a five-story government palace with five domed towers that resembled the Kremlin. Not long after construction began in 1892, architect Henry Hefty realized that he had badly underestimated the cost of the project—budgeted at $500,000—and estimated that it would cost another $500,000 to complete his vision. Hefty was fired, and passersby promenading in adjacent Lownsdale Square clucked at the foundation that sat for a year while city leaders searched for an alternate plan. They eventually selected William H. Whidden, who had overseen construction of the Portland Hotel, and Ion Lewis to take over the project.

The architects' modest redesign, completed in 1895 for $575,000, housed only city administrators (Hefty's plan had also included space for the police department and jail) in a then-futuristic, four-story fireproof building that incorporated innovations like a structural steel skeleton (the city's first), electrical wiring, and public telephones. Inside, Portland's city hall was functional yet elegant, with a French *porte cochère* carriage entrance with Doric columns and a coffered copper ceiling. The ceiling opened onto two light-filled atriums that were tiled in red and white marble and serviced by cast-bronze stairwells (leading to the council chambers and administrative suites) with marble treads. Initial plans called for a 200-foot-tall clock tower, but in keeping with Portland's disdain for ostentation and eschewing the excesses that led to Hefty's firing, the architects wisely left that flourish out of their final drawings.

City Hall's decorative open stairwells were walled off when elevators were added in 1910.

A century after its dedication, City Hall had begun to show its age (the water in the drinking fountains ran yellow, for example), but a two-year renovation in 1996 restored the city's seat to its former glory, opening the main atrium's floor-to-ceiling light courts, which had been closed off for office space in the 1930s.

The newly restored skylit atrium makes City Hall a bright and lively space, even in the gloom of Portland's notoriously gray winters.

The original design for Portland's City Hall called for a palatial building with onion turrets. Deemed too ostentatious (not to mention costly), the city's modest government seat was completed in 1895 with precious little panache, save the entrance rotunda's distinctive pink Scottish Aberdeen granite columns. Today, Portland's understated City Hall stands in stark contrast to its brash, bright-hued neighbor (background, right): Michael Graves's controversial Portland Building.

# MEIER & FRANK BUILDING

Meier & Frank was a family-owned mercantile that Bavarian immigrant Aaron Meier had founded in a 50×30-foot stall on Front Street. In 1907, to celebrate its 50-year anniversary, Meier's son-in-law, Sigmund Frank, took a trip to the Windy City with A. E. Doyle; Frank commissioned the young architect to design an addition to the company's five-story downtown headquarters that would rival Chicago's Carson Pirie Scott Building. When it opened two years later, Meier & Frank's ten-story flagship at the corner of 6th and Alder was the tallest store in the Pacific Northwest. Meier & Frank called itself "Portland's Own Store" and defined the downtown shopping experience for more than half a century, luring legions with a ninth-floor deli, creamery, and grocery, along with ever-more-elaborate novelties such as a sumptuous tenth-floor dining room called the Georgian Room and an auditorium for fashion shows. A fifth-floor radio station began broadcasting in 1922—the same year an itinerant young actor who called himself "Billy" (William Clark Gable) sold neckties in men's accessories.

Like most major department stores across the country, Meier & Frank's fortunes waned in the 1960s as shoppers took their business to suburban malls, and the store was sold off several times. By the time Federated Department Stores took ownership in 2005, Meier & Frank's downtown flagship was in shambles. To its credit, Federated began an ambitious makeover, restoring much of Meier & Frank's luster. But in the process, Portland's Own Store lost its name (to Macy's), and the upper nine floors of the store—including the Georgian Room and the auditorium—were given over to a luxury hotel called the Nines, which opened just before the Christmas season in 2008.

Meier & Frank started out as a mercantile in 1857 and moved into this 5-story, 120,000-square-foot building in 1898 (pictured in the early 1900s).

In 1913, a steam shovel excavates the foundation of a 15-story replacement for Meier & Frank's 1898 building on 5th Avenue between Morrison and Alder streets; when completed, it would become the largest department store west of Chicago.

## Meier & Frank Construction

Masons add glazed white terra-cotta bricks to the façade of the new building, under construction here in 1914, as seen from 5th Avenue, facing Morrison Street. Meier & Frank's new flagship dwarfed a 1909 addition by Doyle, visible from the rear in the background at left. The two buildings were consolidated in 1932, when the store built a final annex (replacing the four-story Morrison Street building at far left) and grew to occupy the entire city block.

## THE SANTALAND MONORAIL

NOBODY IS QUITE SURE WHEN IT HAPPENED (some say '52, others insist '59), or who did it (most likely an Iowa company that built similar Supertrack monorails), but at some point in the 1950s, a kiddie monorail was installed on the ceiling of the tenth floor auditorium of the Meier & Frank Building. Every Christmas for five decades, the rickety sheet-metal contraption resembling a Flash Gordon rocket ship, with its stream-lined nose and tail fins, rattled and clanked through the skies of the store's Santaland display. Every day, from Thanksgiving until Christmas Eve, two-dozen cherubic faces waved to the parents and shouted their Christmas wishes to Santa, seated on his throne in the middle of the room, before the airborne train disappeared into a dramatically lit grotto called the Snow Cave...and emerged a few minutes later with a fresh load of children. The Santaland Monorail took its last flight on Christmas Eve 2005.

### Meier & Frank Completion

This postcard portrays the building after its completion in 1915. Doyle's choice of glazed white terra-cotta was likely influenced by the year he spent in New York City in 1903, working for Henry Bacon, the architect who designed the Lincoln Memorial.

## The Nines

In 2005, Federated Department Stores acquired the Meier & Frank Building *(left)* and sold the upper nine floors to the White Plains, New York–based, Starwood Hotels & Resorts Worldwide. The makeover of Portland's landmark retail space concluded three years later with the unveiling of the Nines, a 331-room boutique hotel with 13 luxurious penthouse suites, which opened atop a remodeled six-story department store, rechristened Macy's at Meier & Frank Square. A steakhouse called the Urban Farmer *(above)* now serves as the centerpiece of the airy, sky-lit atrium of the Nines, a space once occupied by Meier & Frank's stately Georgian Room restaurant and ballroom.

Pioneer Courthouse Square takes its name from Pioneer Courthouse, which stands on the Square's eastern perimeter. Shown here in 1878, nine years after its construction, the location of the building (which also housed the city's post office) was cause for complaint because of its placement on the western-most outskirts of the city.

Railroad tycoon Henry Villard started construction of the Portland Hotel to house travelers appearing due to the arrival of the transcontinental railroad in 1883. After Villard went bankrupt in 1884, the hotel's foundation sat for five years, known as "Villard's ruins," before a group of investors raised the $1 million required to finish the project. When it opened in 1890, the Portland Hotel was one of the largest and most elegant hotels on the West Coast. Pictured here in 1910, guests entered a courtyard that was "adorned in the middle thereof with a circular plat of rare and beautiful shrubbery." The rooftop observation tower afforded "panoramas of far-reaching splendor and unapproachable grandeur spread out for the delectation of guests," as described by an 1891 promotional brochure.

# PIONEER COURTHOUSE SQUARE

In 1849, a shoemaker named Elijah Hill acquired the city block that is now occupied by Pioneer Courthouse Square for $24 and a pair of boots. Like the bartered paper clip that, after a series of ingenious trades, ultimately ends up netting its owner a house, the block underwent many transformations over the next century and a half. It became the city's first public school campus in 1858; a luxury hotel for transcontinental railroad travelers in 1890; a parking lot for Meier & Frank shoppers in 1951; and finally, in 1984, it ended up as "a downtown living room for the people of Portland." That was when the city, in an attempt to revive its crumbling urban core, unveiled the masterwork of an unknown local landscape architect named Willard Martin. He sculpted the parking lot into a vast brick amphitheater where pedestrians—buskers and hucksters, chief executives, commut-

ers, suburbanite shoppers, and street preachers—could mingle and linger. It was a bustling hive of public open space that in 1986 became the Grand Central Station of Portland's futuristic people-mover: the light rail train known as MAX, the Metropolitan Area Express. "Pioneer Courthouse Square is one of the first in a new generation of public squares," wrote Project For Public Spaces, a New York nonprofit urban planning and design organization. In 2005, it ranked Pioneer Courthouse Square third among the nation's great public spaces, after Jackson Square in New Orleans and Manhattan's Rockefeller Plaza. "No longer just passive green spaces, these squares are designed to be programmed and used by the public... The revitalization of downtown is testimony to the square's profound impact on the livability of Portland."

The Portland Hotel (shown here on July 22, 1948) had reached its nadir in the 1940s, when it was purchased by Meier & Frank.

On August 28, 1951, the Portland Hotel hosted a going-away party: A public auction sold off everything from gilded china to Teddy Roosevelt's bed (which went for $500) to monogrammed bath towels. It was an ignominious end for what was once the city's most glamorous address.

Meier & Frank razed the Portland Hotel in 1951 and built a parking lot (pictured in the 1970s), an eyesore at the heart of downtown Portland for 30 years.

In 1981, the city purchased the Meier & Frank parking lot and demolished it to build a central piazza modeled after European public squares.

## PORTLAND'S LIVING ROOM

When the city sent out its call for proposals for the design of Pioneer Courthouse Square in 1980, 162 architectural firms from around the world submitted entries. Local architect Willard K. Martin, a self-described artist/humorist/inventor/sociologist, was the dark horse of the finalists, but his concept for Pioneer Courthouse Square prevailed. Martin intended the square itself to serve as a museum, incorporating found objects tied to the history of the place—such as the front gate of the demolished Portland Hotel—and artwork. In order to offset the cost of the project, 50,000 bricks were sold to the public. The bricks, which were inscribed with the purchaser's name, were then used to create the square. The venture raised $750,000 for construction. Martin, who coined the term "Portland's Living Room" to describe the project's utility, tragically died in an airplane crash a year after the square was dedicated in 1984. A bronze of his trademark broad-rimmed Dutch hat rests atop a lectern overlooking the Square's main amphitheater.

This is one of architect Willard Martin's early sketches of Pioneer Courthouse Square. The gazebo-like structure in the middle is a pulpit, one of his favorite whimsical features, which ultimately was built without a roof.

One of the Square's most compelling landmarks is the Portland Hotel's wrought-iron main entrance gate. It was salvaged when the hotel was demolished in 1951 and reinstalled on the Square's eastern perimeter in 1984, in the spot where it once stood—a memorial to a lost civic treasure.

Pioneer Courthouse Square gets a summertime makeover every June as the venue for the city's Festival of Flowers, pictured here in 2007. This image was taken at the height of a reconstruction of the upper floors of the Meier & Frank Building, as evidenced by the service elevator and scaffolding affixed to the building's 6th Avenue façade. The steel skeleton of what will become the atrium and penthouses of the Nines luxury hotel also is visible in the background.

Aside from being a popular destination for downtown office workers, Pioneer Courthouse Square stages hundreds of civic events each year, from the lighting of the city's towering Douglas fir Christmas tree in December to summertime celebrations such as Sand in the City, when the Square becomes a sandbox, with 450 tons of beach trucked in from the Oregon coast, used for a citywide sculpting competition. In 2008, the American Planning Association named Pioneer Courthouse Square, along with New York City's Central Park and Washington, D.C.'s Union Station, as one of the nation's great public spaces.

Portland residents, who purchased engraved bricks to help fund the Square's construction, search for their names embedded in the Square's brick amphitheater on opening day, April 6, 1984. The lectern from Martin's sketch can be seen over the grottolike entrance to a theater and information center.

A whimsical milepost imbues the Square with a sense of place.

Every day at noon, a mechanical clock called *The Weather Machine* trumpets "Fanfare for the Common Man" as a weather vane emerges from its stainless crown to predict the day's forecast. Here, a Helia indicates another cloudless summer day.

## A Square of Sculptures

*Allow Me (right)* has become one of the most-photographed sculptures in the square, but as shown at left, the square itself is a sculpture.

*The Whispering Chamber,* an acoustic sculpture carved into the Square's northwest corner, is a favorite gathering place for chess players during the summer. The dark panels inset into the uppermost tier of the bowl-shape mini amphitheater tell the story of the many transitions the square has undergone since shoemaker Elijah Hill acquired the property in 1849. Since then, it has progressed from a public school campus to hotel grounds to a parking lot, until it was finally recast as one of the nation's most lauded piazzas.

# BROADWAY

By the time 7th Avenue's name was changed to Broadway with the dedication of the Broadway Bridge in 1913, the thoroughfare had already established itself as downtown's liveliest strip, the daytime knots of well-mannered shoppers and office drones giving way in the evenings to a boisterous crowd of theatergoers out for a carefree night on the town. In the 1920s and '30s, the stately vaudeville playhouses that had risen on the southern half of Broadway—the Baker, the Orpheum, the Heilig, the Liberty—were converted to cavernous cinemas that competed for customers (the largest boasted more than 3,000 seats) with ever-more-elaborately lighted marquees and displays. For a time, as historian E. Kimbark MacColl notes in *The Growth of a City,* Portland's Great White Way rivaled Manhattan's. In 1926, the journal *American City* singled out Broadway as "one of the best-lighted streets in America."

"By day, downtown Portland was still a conventional shopping and business district," Portland-raised *Rolling Stone* editor Mikal Gilmore wrote in his 1994 memoir, *Shot in the Heart.* "By night, though, downtown Portland changed its character. Along the main drag of Broadway there was a strip of bustling bars and restaurants, and many of them stayed open all night. Inside these spots, you could find an interesting late-night social life: a mix of Portland's rich folks and aspiring bohemians, plus a colorful smattering of its would-be criminal types."

Although the street lost much of its wattage when theaters closed in the 1960s and '70s due to multiplexes opening in the suburbs, Broadway remains the city's official "neon district" and the heart of downtown nightlife. During the day, it's also a destination for shoppers, although much of the bag-toting foot traffic shifted two blocks to the east in 1990, with the opening of downtown's primary mall, Pioneer Place.

Not long after opening in 1928, the 3,000-seat Portland Publix Theatre changed the name on its 65-tall neon marquee to the Paramount. By 1948, when *Unfaithfully Yours* was screening at the Paramount, the vaudeville theaters along Broadway Avenue had been converted to movie houses and competed for customers with ever-increasing wattage.

## Bustling Broadway

For more than half a century, Charles F. Berg's women's boutique at the corner of Morrison and Broadway (pictured above in the late 1940s) was the city's epicenter of couture, employing a team of high school and college-age trend spotters and staging an annual fashion show. The store's Tiffany elevator and women's lounge (designed to evoke Catalina's Submarine Gardens) disappeared when the store closed in 1983, but the building's lavish Art Deco terra-cotta façade, embellished with 18-karat gold leaf, remains as a testament to the street's spare-no-expense former prominence.

*Right:* This present-day scene, in front of the 1913 Morgan Building on Broadway at Washington, is one block north of the former Charles F. Berg's. It has less foot traffic due to the opening of Pioneer Place, downtown's largest shopping mall. However, a few of the old stores have stuck it out: Three blocks south, at the corner of Broadway and Salmon, John Helmer III still sells fedoras out of the eponymous haberdashery his grandfather opened in 1921, when Rudolph Valentino's *The Sheik* was screening at the Orpheum just up the street.

A postcard of the corner of SW Broadway and Main shows the Portland Publix Theatre in 1937, when its name was the Paramount.

# ARLENE SCHNITZER CONCERT HALL

When the Portland Publix Theatre opened at the corner of SW Broadway and Main on March 8, 1928, it lived up to an advertisement that had promised "a worthy addition to the palaces of this world." It had a six-story marquee with 6,000 incandescent bulbs and 1,000 feet of neon tubing (then reportedly the largest neon sign in the world); regally appointed lobbies adorned with tapestries, paintings, grand pianos, suits of armor, and two magnificent crystal chandeliers; and a cavernous auditorium with more than an acre of seats and a thousand-pipe organ with twin keyboards. The Portland was palatial in every respect. On opening night, some 3,000 Portlanders paid 60 cents apiece to attend the debut show, including an organ recital and a screening of *Feel My Pulse,* a silent comedy about a hypochondriac who inherits an insane asylum.

By 1972, however, time, television, and suburban cineplexes had taken their toll: Only 60 of the 3,000 seats were sold for the venue's final screening, *Dr. Phibes Rises Again,* a Vincent Price horror film. Three years later, faced with mounting losses, the crumbling building's owner auctioned off everything of value, including the pipe organ, which was carted away by a Denver pizza parlor. The city condemned the building in 1982, but Portlanders—still smarting from the loss of the Portland Hotel 30 years earlier—rallied. They taxed themselves to the tune of $19 million and held fundraisers that included selling $25 Portland Theater marquee lapel pins to pay for a full-scale renovation of the downtown landmark. It reopened in 1984 as the Arlene Schnitzer Concert Hall (named for a patron who literally paid a fortune for her lapel pin) and became the new home of the Portland Symphony Orchestra.

## Restored to Glory

The 1982 renovation of the Arlene Schnitzer Concert Hall (called "The Schnitz" by locals) restored the venue's 65-foot-tall marquee to the theater's original name. Today, the landmark is the home of the Portland Symphony Orchestra.

Founded in 1892, the Portland Art Museum is the oldest art museum on the west coast. The latest addition to the museum's 1932 South Park Blocks campus, the Mark Building (shown above), houses the Jubitz Center for Modern & Contemporary Art, the largest modern art exhibition space in the region. The three-story sculpture visible in the foreground is Roy Lichtenstein's *Brushstrokes*.

# PORTLAND ART MUSEUM

Founded as the Portland Art Association in 1892, the oldest art museum on the West Coast began with a modest collection of 100 plaster reproductions of classic Greek and Roman sculptures that were housed in the city's public library. In 1930, the benefactor who had donated those plaster statues, Winslow B. Ayer, bequeathed $100,000 to the museum to build a permanent home. Anna Belle Crocker was the museum's second curator—and a controversial curator at that. She created a sensation by being the first to exhibit Duchamp's *Nude Descending A Staircase* after the 1913 New York Armory Show. She made an equally bold statement by

championing the work of a young maverick, Pietro Belluschi, a 20-something apprentice architect from Italy whose drawings had caught Crocker's eye. The Portland Art Museum was Belluschi's first major commission, and the design he proposed represented a radical departure from the past—a sleek low-slung, two-story rectangular block of red brick with horizontal windows. The board objected, demanding a classical—and monumental—Georgian building. But Belluschi persisted and enlisted the help of Frank Lloyd Wright, who, after reviewing Belluschi's sketches, wrote a letter to the board extolling the merits of the young architect's design, which was ultimately approved. When

the Portland Art Museum was unveiled in 1932, it was heralded as the first Modernist gallery in America and propelled Belluschi's adopted city onto the national stage as a place that embraces the unconventional.

"The museum is in a deep sense the mirror of the civilization which built it," Belluschi told an interviewer in 1984. "A modern and alive museum, at least in this country, does not merely collect old paintings for the sake of showing how wealthy a city it is... The museum's most important mission is furnishing the means of restoring aesthetics to their normal relation to the other human activities."

On January 18, 1934, spotlights draw crowds to a Chevrolet auto show at the Masonic Temple adjacent to the newly opened Portland Art Museum. The museum later acquired the building and made it the centerpiece of a $40-million expansion in 2005.

Manuel Izquierdo's *Eye of Orion,* a gift of philanthropists Harold and Arlene Schnitzer, stands in the Evan Roberts Memorial Sculpture Garden outside the Mark Building. The Mark Building opened in 2005 to house the museum's modern art collection—the sleek glass panels that embellish the former Masonic Temple's otherwise staid façade suggests as much.

Landscape architect Lawrence Halprin wowed New York City art critics with Forecourt Fountain, pictured here after its 1970 dedication. "It could be called environmental sculpture or environmental art . . . Mr. Halprin is on to something that makes the conventional piece of modern sculpture plonked onto the conventional corporate or public plaza look obsolete," *The New York Times* art critic Ada Louise Huxtable wrote. "He has rediscovered . . . what made the Fontana dei Trevi, for example, or the Piazza Navona, work . . . They were 'people plazas.'"

# FORECOURT FOUNTAIN

As part of its South Auditorium urban-renewal project in the late 1960s, the city approved a proposal by the San Francisco–based landscape architect Lawrence Halprin for a public park fountain across the street from its newly renovated Civic Auditorium. Halprin had won international accolades for a faux mountain stream called Lovejoy Fountain that he created for a nearby apartment-building courtyard in 1965. Like Olin Warner's 1885 Skidmore Fountain, a functional work of art that doubled as a water trough, Halprin intended Forecourt Fountain to be seen but also to be used by the public—in this case, as an urban swimming hole meant to evoke the cascading waterfalls found in the nearby Columbia River Gorge. Like Skidmore Fountain, Forecourt Fountain impressed the New York City art establishment and left it wondering how Portland had pulled off such a coup. A few days before the fountain was turned on in 1970, Halprin gave a preview to *The New York Times* architecture critic Ada Louise Huxtable, who lamented the fact that Portland, and not Manhattan, had been the recipient of such a seminal work, advising readers that "for now, to see the best, go West."

### Bathing Suits, not Business Suits

The park is meant to attract visitors who want to relax and have fun. Its fountain brings a sense of the cascading waterfalls found in the nearby Columbia River Gorge to the inner city: 13,000 gallons of water per minute flow into pools that hold more than 75,000 gallons of water.

# SOUTH PARK BLOCKS

A trip to Europe inspired Daniel Lownsdale, an early Portland landowner, to donate a string of lots between Salmon and Hall streets that would forever be "dedicated to public use." Simply known as the South Park Blocks, Lownsdale's donation, located a half mile from the river, remained a stump-covered mud roadway until 1877, when the city council authorized florist and landscape designer Louis G. Pfunder to plant poplars and elms. By 1885, when the city appointed an official park keeper, the Park Blocks served as Portland's version of Central Park— a leafy swath of green surrounded on all sides by stately mansions. As the expanding commercial district grew up around the Park Blocks, the mansions were replaced by theaters, hotels, and cultural institutions such as the Portland Art Museum, which moved to the Park Blocks in 1932.

The Vanport Extension Center was a community college for Kaiser shipyard workers and returning veterans that had been destroyed when a flood inundated the upriver city of Vanport. In 1952, it moved into Lincoln High School, which had been relocated to a modern campus a half-dozen blocks to the west. The school grew up around the Blocks. In 1955, it changed its name to Portland State College when it began offering a four-year degree program. The South Park Blocks served as the school's quad and became a gathering place for student anti-war protests and demonstrations during the turbulent 1960s. In 1969, its name was changed again, this time to Portland State University. With an enrollment of more than 24,000, PSU is the largest university in the state. Today, the Blocks is a tranquil place, shaded by the now-giant poplars and elms planted more than 130 years ago. It's a popular hangout for students, a destination for concert and museum goers, and home to the city's largest outdoor farmer's market, the Portland Farmer's Market, attracting swarms of shoppers to browse the bounty of the Willamette valley on brilliant Saturdays during the summer.

Wearing helmets and padded clothing to protect themselves from riot police, Portland State students take their protest to the streets of downtown in 1969. During the 1960s, the South Park Blocks often served as a staging ground for student-led anti-war demonstrations.

On March 26, 1968, ten days after declaring his candidacy for the presidency and three months before his assassination, Senator Robert F. Kennedy addresses a crowd of adoring Portland State College students.

The former home of lumber baron Simon Benson was relocated from the corner of SW 11th and Clay to the South Park Blocks on January 16, 2000. The dilapidated 100-year-old Queen Anne–style residence—previously used as a boarding house and condemned by the city in 1991—was rescued from demolition and moved to the campus of Portland State University.

The restored Simon Benson House now serves as the home of Portland State's alumni association and the school's visitor reception center. Notice the four-bowled Benson Bubbler (one of the original 20 public drinking fountains Benson donated in 1912) on the sidewalk at the foot of the front porch. It also sits on a busy South Park Blocks corner that plays host to the city's largest outdoor farmer's market. Every weekend, farmers, beekeepers, butchers, vintners, fishmongers, artisan bakers, and cheese makers from across the Willamette Valley draw thousands of shoppers to their produce stalls.

# CENTRAL LIBRARY

Portland's public library was founded as a subscription library in 1864, when a group of downtown merchants pooled their money and mail-ordered $2,000 ($27,000 today) worth of classics from a New York City bookseller. For the first five years, the collection was located at 66 Southwest 1st Street, but eventually, it relocated to a rented 24×80-foot, sky-lit room above the Ladd & Tilton Bank on 1st and Stark, where it remained for 24 years.

With a $5,000 gift from pharmacist Stephen Skidmore, who died in 1883, the Portland Library Association commissioned a Boston architect to design a permanent home for its growing collection of more than 21,000 volumes. Completed in 1894, the two-story library at 7th Avenue and Stark Street was simple yet elegant, modeled after the Boston Public Library, with the stacks on the main floor off a central corridor, a second-floor lecture hall, and a gallery for the Portland Art Museum upstairs. When downtown merchant John Wilson died in 1900, he bequeathed a collection of more than 8,000 rare volumes, with the stipulation that the Library Association make the collection available to the public for free. After levying a city-wide tax in 1911, the Association raised $450,000 ($9.7 million today) for a new three-story home, which would be one of the most important—and most visited—commissions of local architect A. E. Doyle's career. In 2006, the Multnomah County Public Library system's 370,000 patrons borrowed an average of 52 books each, making Portland's library the second most used library in the nation.

Central Library's main entrance is shown here in April 1936. When the building was dedicated in 1913, architect A.E. Doyle said that he intentionally kept the design simple.

The formal attire and studious fervor of the patrons in this photo, circa 1913, adds to the collegiate atmosphere of the Technical Room on the second floor of Central Library. "Many years ago the public library was called the 'University of the people'; an apt phrase today, for these shelves point the way to self-education, their volumes offer the means of the broadest culture or of special training," said chief librarian Mary Isom at the building's dedication on September 6, 1913. "The public library is the people's library, it is maintained by the people for the people, it is the most democratic of our democratic institutions."

Of all the downtown buildings that architect A. E. Doyle designed, the city's Central Library consistently ranks as the public's favorite—it was also Doyle's favorite. "When an architect gets a library job he is naturally very enthusiastic about it and considers it the big chance he has been waiting for," Doyle said at the library's 1913 dedication. "His uppermost thought is to make it a monument."

Doyle made ample use of natural light for the library's interior. Here, a skylight illuminates the third floor's main staircase.

# STREETCARS

After selling his San Francisco stagecoach franchise to Wells Fargo for $1.5 million (approximately $23 million today) in 1868, California entrepreneur Benjamin Holladay moved to Portland and gave $10,000 of his fortune to the city's first public transportation system, the Portland Street Railway Company. It began operating in 1872, with a secondhand San Francisco trolley, an ornery mule, and surplus track from Holladay's Oregon & California Railroad (the first in Oregon). Service was slow, but the franchise grew to 11 cars and 35 horses, and copycats followed. When the Portland Railway, Light and Power Company consolidated the city's 28 separately owned streetcar lines in 1906, Portland's electric-trolley network—with a fleet of more than 375 cars providing 60 million trips per year over 160 miles of track—was one of the largest public transportation systems in the nation.

In the 1920s, instead of laying down new track, the company began tearing rails out of the streetbed as it replaced its fleet of aging trolleys with more economical diesel-powered buses and electric "trackless trolleys." Electric streetcar ridership peaked briefly during World War II due to fuel rationing, but the revival was short-lived. By 1949, the Portland Traction Company (the transportation arm of the old electric company) had nearly 500 buses and only 38 streetcars. On February 26, 1950, the last streetcar in Portland was carted off to the scrapyard. Then something interesting happened. As car ownership increased and public transportation ridership waned, people stopped walking, and Portland's downtown deteriorated. Looking to the future, city planners revived a relic from the city's past. In 1986, for the first time in a generation, a trolley began rumbling along Portland's streets: the Metropolitan Area Express, a line connecting downtown with the suburbs of Hillsboro and Gresham. By 2009, the city's fleet of 127 light rail trains was providing 4.5 million trips a year over 33 miles of track. It's a far cry from Portland's electric streetcar heyday, but in 137 years, the city has come a long way from Ben Holladay's secondhand trolley and mule.

In 1872, a round trip on Portland's first street car—a mule-powered San Francisco trolley that ran the length of 1st Street—took an hour. By 1893, the Transcontinental Street Railway Company retired its last mule-driven car (pictured here) as electric streetcars began whisking riders up into the hills and the hinterlands across the river.

By the end of World War II, the popularity of gasoline-powered buses and electric "trackless trolleys" doomed Portland's streetcar system. Here, three castoff cars are burnt for scrap on August 17, 1948. Two years later, streetcars, which had been part of the city's fabric for nearly eight decades, had vanished from the streets of Portland.

After trolley service to the Council Crest neighborhood was discontinued, an old car was returned by truck on November 21, 1950. The car stayed on exhibit in Council Crest Park until it was badly vandalized. It is now in the Oregon Electric Railway Museum in Brooks, Oregon.

After a hiatus of nearly four decades, in 1986, the city's back-to-the-futuristic Metropolitan Express light rail trains began shuttling commuters through the heart of downtown on a 33-mile line stretching from the suburbs of Hillsboro to Gresham.

In 1999, workers lay track for the Portland Streetcar, a 4.8-mile, north-south oriented downtown people mover augmenting the city's mostly east-west oriented light rail network, which began operating in 2001.

# BICYCLES

At the turn of the century, entrepreneur Fred T. Merrill was Portland's bicycling king. Not only could he ride—he won the state bicycling championship in 1884 at a downtown velodrome—but Merrill, a city councilman from 1899 to 1905, was singlehandedly responsible for the city's bicycle craze at the turn of the century. As historian E. Kimbark MacColl notes in *A Shaping of a City*, in 1898, the Fred T. Merrill Cycle Co. sold 8,850 bicycles, making Merrill's 2,000 square-foot downtown showroom the largest bike dealership west of the Mississippi. In 1899, the council required cyclists to purchase and display $1.25 license tags on their cycles. The fad died with the automobile, however—the first car in Portland arrived in 1898. By 1905, the number multiplied to 218 and grew exponentially after that, to the point that even Fred T. Merrill ultimately closed his bicycle shop and started selling Fords.

Bicycles began to multiply on city streets again in the 1980s and 1990s as part of the city's pedestrian-friendly downtown makeover. The makeover encouraged amenities for cyclists including bicycle lanes, bicycle racks, and incentives for office tower developers to provide changing rooms and showers. In 1995, and again in 1999, *Bicycling* magazine named Portland the most bicycling-friendly city in the nation.

"People take bicycles more seriously in Portland than in any other U.S. city, which is why it's our top American city for the second time," wrote *Bicycling*. "Must be something about the smell of pine, rain-washed air and verdant hills. Bikes are part of the whole 'green' package here."

A downtown bicycle commuter is shown here circa 1900. As historian Perry Maddox writes in his 1952 history of Portland, *City on the Willamette*, so many cyclists clogged the city's streets, dodging pedestrians, streetcars, and carriages, that the city council considered adopting an ordinance that would require a lane for bicycles on every fifth east-west street.

In 1995, a nonprofit called the Community Cycling Center began leaving dozens of bright yellow public bicycles around the city that people could borrow for short trips, and then leave for the next user. The experiment ultimately proved to be a failure—by 2000, so many yellow bicycles had vanished that the program was discontinued.

A bicyclist crosses downtown's Broadway Bridge. In 2008, bicycles accounted for 14 percent of all vehicular traffic on the bridge and 20 percent of traffic on the Hawthorne crossing. Data from the U.S. Census Bureau's 2005 American Community Survey shows that Portland has more bicycle commuters than any other big city—eight times the national average.

In downtown Portland, bicycles have become part of the cityscape. A city ordinance requires all new developments to set aside spaces for bicycle parking and provides incentives for developers to include showers and locker rooms for bicycle commuters.

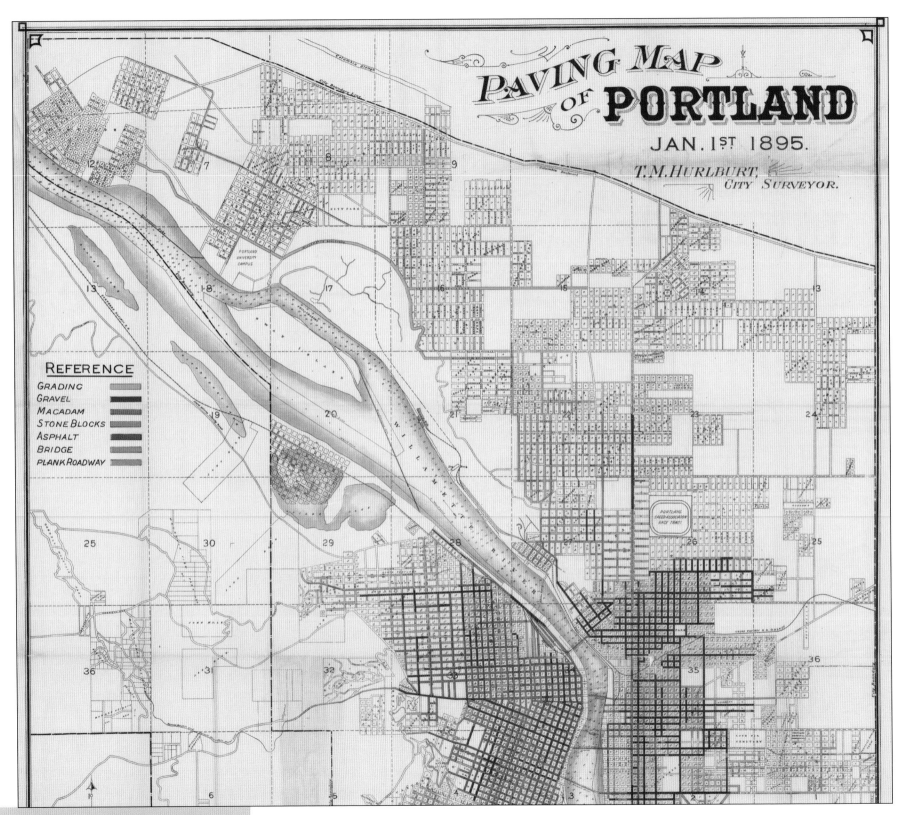

PAVING MAP OF PORTLAND
JAN. 1ST 1895.

T. M. HURLBURT,
CITY SURVEYOR.

REFERENCE
GRADING
GRAVEL
MACADAM
STONE BLOCKS
ASPHALT
BRIDGE
PLANK ROADWAY

# THE CITY'S CAPTAIN

Oregon City's prominence may have endured if John Heard Couch (rhymes with "pooch"), a swarthy New England seafarer who wore gold hoop earrings, hadn't dropped anchor in Portland in 1845, declaring, "To this very point, to this exact point I can bring any ship that can get into the mouth of the Columbia River. And not, sir, a rod further."

So convinced of the superior position Portland commanded on the Willamette—situated in deep water devoid of shoals and shallows—he claimed the square mile adjacent to the Pettygrove/Lovejoy tract as his own. Couch's Addition, as Northwest Portland then was known, extended from the hills to the west down to the riverfront, where Couch built a warehouse and a wharf before setting out to sea.

In 1850, after voyaging to Hong Kong and Manila, the 39-year-old mariner from Newburyport, Massachusetts, docked one last time, founded a downtown shipping line, and made Portland his home. On the site of present-day Union Station, a few blocks from the waterfront, Couch built a fine one-story house with a broad columned porch that faced a vast shallow lake covering 40 city blocks. There he lived out his days, contentedly shooting at mallards from the comfort of a rocking chair.

## C FOR COUCH

In April 1851, after enduring the two-month voyage from Philadelphia (which involved a three-day transit on muleback between the Atlantic and Pacific at the isthmus of Panama), John B. Preston, Oregon Territory's first surveyor general, sailed past the newly incorporated city of Portland and settled 13 miles downriver with his wife and daughter in Oregon

Captain John Heard Couch is pictured here with his wife, Caroline. Captain Couch, a Massachusetts mariner, sailed into Portland harbor on the *Chenamus*, opened a store in Oregon City, and three years later claimed a square mile of land now known as Northwest Portland. Just inland from the wharf he erected along the waterfront, Couch built a house on the edge of a lake, then finally, 13 years after arriving in Portland, sent for his wife and children.

*Left:* This 1895 paving map demonstrates how the grid of Couch's Addition (on the west bank of the river, lower left, which is present-day Northwest Portland) differentiates itself from the grid of downtown Portland. According to historian Eugene Snyder, mariner John Heard Couch oriented the streets in his subdivision to true north, using the North Star as a reference. "It is pleasant to imagine that Couch, careful navigator that he was, liked the idea of using the ever-constant North Star as his target," Snyder wrote in *Portland Names and Neighborhoods: Their Historic Origins.*

City. At the time, Oregon City was the seat of the territory's government and seemed destined—poised as it was on a bluff overlooking Willamette Falls—to remain Oregon's foremost city.

On June 7, 1851, Preston marched to the western edge of Couch's claim and, shouldering his surveying instruments, bushwhacked to the summit of the forested hills. At that spot he drove a wooden stake, from which he began mapping all of the land claims and town sites that had been filed in Oregon Country. But Couch didn't make the job easy for him.

Couch platted his streets as he sailed the seas, using celestial true north. The end result: On a clear night he could look down any north-aligned street in his claim and see Polaris, the North Star, shining above B Street (present-day Burnside), the primary east-west boulevard that separated his tract from the Pettygrove/Lovejoy claim. The plat Couch submitted had no named streets, just numbers for those that ran north-south and letters for east-west. The city subsequently amended this in 1891 by naming the lettered streets in Couch's Addition after prominent Portlanders, with C, naturally, reserved for Couch.

## COUCH'S INHABITANTS

The upper quadrant of Couch's Addition—an enclave that is still known as the Alphabet District—attracted the city's upper crust. They built more than a few marble-clad mansions and Victorian walk-ups with gingerbread sheathing, but the wharves and warehouses of the lower half of the Couch tract appealed to a decidedly downscale clientele. Thanks in large part to the sway Couch held in seaports around the globe, Portland had become one of the busiest ports of call on the West Coast by the end of the 19th century, and the foot of Couch's Addition was where the sailors chose to spend their money. The North End, present-day Old Town, became famous across the Pacific and beyond for its brothels, boarding houses, opium dens, and most of all, its pubs. Erickson's Saloon was a shrine to devotees of the alcoholic arts. They hoisted mugs of Weinhard's ale (brewed just a few blocks away) from a 684-foot mahogany bar, billed as the world's longest, that encircled its perimeter.

A warehouse district served as a buffer zone between the Alphabet District and the North End until the 1980s, when the area was colonized by artists and gallery owners. The stage was set for the area's rebirth as the Pearl District, an ever-expanding vertical neighborhood of luxury condominiums, boutiques, and upscale restaurants serviced by a streetcar line that connected the neighborhood with downtown's light rail network. In 2003, the city commissioned Atelier Dreiseitl, a renowned German landscape architecture firm, to sculpt a water park on a vacant lot that had once been a railyard—artificial wetlands called Tanner Springs. Evoking Tanner Creek, which once ambled across the Couch claim and fed Couch Lake, a humanmade stream

Willamette Stone State Park was named for a stone obelisk that, in 1885, replaced the wooden stake that surveyor John B. Preston drove into the ground. After vandals stole the stone in the 1980s, the landmark was replaced with a brass geological survey marker, along with a plaque (pictured here) that can be found at the end of a short trail off Southwest Skyline Boulevard.

trickles from one corner of the park and empties into a pond.

The pond represents Couch Lake, which disappeared when it was filled for the city's train depot and main post office three years after the captain died of pneumonia in 1870. Unlike Jamison Square Park—another green space two blocks south with a waterfall that attracts hordes of children in the summer— Tanner Springs is a contemplative space, where couples stroll hand in hand and Canada geese strut on the grass and swim in the pond. You can almost sense the spirit of Captain Couch surveying the scene from one of the many balconies bordering the park on all sides, kicking back in his rocking chair, boots on the rail and a shotgun cradled in his lap, contentment etched across his face.

### Tanner Springs Park

In 2004, the city broke ground on German landscape architect Herbert Dreiseitl's Tanner Springs Park *(above)*, a wetlands-themed green space carved among the high-rise luxury condominium towers built atop a former rail yard near Union Station. The park was named for Tanner Creek, which once flowed through Couch's Addition from the West Hills and was channeled into the city's sewer system in the late 1800s. A humanmade stream burbles from the ground in the center of the park and empties into a pond. It is meant to evoke the former Couch Lake, which once covered the area; the rusted railroad track that forms a wall on the eastern edge of the artificial lake *(right)* dates from 1898 and recalls Northern Pacific's once sprawling—now vanished—switchyard.

# THE WATERFRONT

According to historian Eugene Snyder, Captain John Heard Couch partnered with his brother-in-law, Massachusetts mariner George Flanders, in 1864, and threw open the doors of the Gulley & Condon. Being business-savvy seamen, they strategically located their watering hole on the riverfront, at the corner of Front Street and B, within stumbling distance of their primary investment property—Portland's largest dock, which spanned three blocks of the riverfront from B through D streets. Couch's wharf wasn't a pretty place, and it attracted downscale patrons: the outcasts of Portland society, from merchant mariners to Chinese laborers to down-on-their luck transients who squatted in half-sunken wrecks beached on the riverbank. By the late 19th century, the lower half of Couch's Addition was known as the North End, and no respectable Portlander would be found there. As legend has it, crimps like Joseph Bunco Kelly and boxer/flophouse owner Larry Sullivan haunted the docks, selling comatose drunks into service aboard cargo ships. Then there were miscreants like Nancy Boggs, a frequent target of reformist ire and police raids. She operated a whiskey scow that writer Stewart Holbrook described as "a floating hellhole." Harvey Scott, in his definitive *History of Portland*, walked the streets of the city in 1890 and gave Couch's North End a wide berth, describing it from a distance as an "area of mean buildings" that "looks, at present, rather crude and backdoorish."

In the 1890s, the city council renamed B Street—the primary east-west avenue that separated downtown from Couch's Addition—as Burnside, for a respected merchant. However, everyone called the avenue's lower half Skid Road, for rowdy lumbermen and sailors who spent their paychecks there and stumbled into the gutter. Although the Gulley & Condon no longer exists and the Port of Portland has migrated downriver, the former North End waterfront—now called Old Town—retains its image as a haven of last resort for the disenfranchised and remains downtown's rough-and-tumble backdoor. But that's precisely why some cherish the place as an authentic piece of Portland's past.

An ocean-going cargo ship drops anchor in Portland Harbor near the turn of the 19th century. By 1890, Portland was second only to San Francisco as the busiest port on the West Coast, with ships delivering 5,000 passengers and more than 40,000 tons of freight of each month.

One of the better-dressed families (with well-heeled pets trained to truly sit) camped along the west bank of the Willamette (just north of present-day Burnside Bridge) near the turn of the century.

The Portland City Directory of 1889 advertised the Merchants' Hotel at the corner of 3rd and D streets. It was located in the heart of what was then the rough-and-tumble North End (present-day Old Town).

Long after Portlanders of Japanese ancestry were relocated to internment camps at the onset of World War II, the Merchants' Hotel building—which had served as the commercial hub of the neighborhood's Japanese community from the turn of the century until the 1940s—continued as a hotel. The last guests checked out in the 1980s.

Since 1949, the Portland Rescue Mission has catered to the homeless camped in doorways and cardboard boxes along West Burnside Street near the city's waterfront. Burnside has long served as the city's primary east-west boulevard and, near the waterfront in Old Town (the North End), is a magnet for the downtrodden.

# CHINATOWN AND JAPANTOWN

In 1890, Portland's Chinatown, which was centered around a six-block stretch of Southwest 2nd Avenue, was the largest Chinatown in the Northwest and the second largest in the nation (after San Francisco). According to Marie Rose Wong's history of the city's Chinese community, *Sweet Cakes, Long Journey: The Chinatowns of Portland, Oregon,* Chinatown's 4,539 Chinese—mostly male bachelors who came to Portland in search of jobs with railroads, in canneries, and as personal servants—made up a little less than ten percent of the city's population.

*The Oregonian* editor Harvey Scott railed against the "Chinaman disease" in weekly editorials and opined in his 1890 *History of Portland,* "They are not a particularly desirable people and are subject to the usual criticisms and strictures that apply to man in his natural state, but it has not been found necessary to expel them."

Marginalizing them was another story, however. In addition to the Chinese Exclusion Act of 1882, Scott had long urged city leaders to evict the Chinese from the city's center, forcing them into a segregated ghetto district as had been done in San Francisco. Chinese businesses were pushed to a less-desirable, ten-block area of the sordid North End. By the turn of the century, Japanese immigrants began coming to Chinatown while the number of Chinese, as a result

of the Exclusion Act and other factors, plummeted from a high of 7,841 in 1900 to 1,569 by 1940.

During the same period, Chinese businesses clustered along Northwest 4th Avenue, as a new Japantown of more than 100 Japanese-owned businesses emerged on 2nd, 3rd, and 5th avenues, an area also known as "Little Tokyo." But six months after the attack on Pearl Harbor, Japantown ceased to exist overnight as Japanese Americans were dispatched to internment camps, beginning with the Portland Assembly Center in North Portland. All that remained of Portland's once dominant Asian community was its 4th Avenue Chinatown, which was a fraction of its former size.

In the 2000s, after a city-funded streetscape makeover and construction of a new light rail line to Union Station, rent in Chinatown again skyrocketed, forcing longtime Chinatown fixtures, such as Hung Far Low restaurant, to relocate along Southeast 82nd Avenue, a downtrodden boulevard on the city's outermost fringes. In December 2008, *The Oregonian* declared a spruced-up Chinatown to be "Portland's Next Big Thing." It was a prescient statement: Two months later, local wunderkind chef Andy Ricker opened an upscale Asian restaurant called Ping in the spot vacated by Hung Far Low. It was hailed as the culinary event of the year (of the Ox).

From the 1870s until the early 1900s, dozens of Chinese-owned businesses—similar to the grocery pictured above—thrived in the Southwest 2nd Avenue Chinatown. By the turn of the century, the city's Asian community was forced to relocate to less desirable real estate south of West Burnside. A "New Chinatown" business district took root along Northwest 4th Avenue, while a nexus of Japanese-owned businesses ("Japantown") dominated avenues to the east and west. However, in May, 1942, the U.S. government forced the city's Japanese residents into internment camps and Japantown ceased to exist almost overnight as white-owned businesses settled into hastily vacated storefronts.

From the turn of the century until President Franklin Delano Roosevelt passed Executive Order 9066 in February 1942—leading to the internment of people of Japanese ancestry—more than 100 Japanese-owned businesses such as this barbershop/bathhouse/laundry from 1917, were concentrated within an eight-block stretch of present-day Northwest Portland.

Gymnasiums specializing in judo, kendo (fencing), and even sumo wrestling, such as the Portland Sumo boys team pictured here in 1931, were located on Northwest Davis Street between 2nd and 3rd avenues.

## Chinatown Relic

The China Gate, built by artisans from Taiwan and dedicated in 1986, stands at West Burnside and Northwest 4th Avenue, the main strip of the city's Chinatown. The once-thriving business district has shrunk to a fraction of its former size since its heyday in the late 19th century. A streetscape makeover and construction of a new light rail line brought renewed commercial interest to the area. Faced with the prospect of higher rent, many Asian businesses have migrated across the river to the more affordable (but less-desirable) Southeast 82nd Avenue.

## The Tower of Cosmic Reflections

The centerpiece of *Lan Su Yuan,* also known as the Portland Classical Chinese Garden, is an 8,000-square-foot pond called Lake Zither. An assortment of teas and traditional delicacies such as *lo bo gao* (turnip cakes) and *mang gong* (rice flour cookies) are served on the second floor of the garden's ceremonial teahouse, the Tower of Cosmic Reflections. The tower, true to its name, is mirrored on the surface of Lake Zither.

# UNION STATION

In the 1870s, railroad tycoon Henry Villard filled Couch Lake and hired the New York City architects who designed Manhattan's Pennsylvania Station to draw up plans for a Grand Union Depot (which Villard intended to be the largest train station in the world) to serve as the western terminus for the transcontinental railroad he was bankrolling to Portland. The link arrived in East Portland in 1883, followed by a new Willamette River crossing, the Steel Bridge, in 1888, but Villard went bankrupt before he could break ground on his new depot. Northern Pacific Railroad took over the project and hired Henry Van Brunt, the architect of the Union Passenger Station in Worcester, Massachusetts, to execute a scaled-back redesign, which called for a structure that would have been at home in Renaissance Florence: a palazzo with a red-brick and stucco façade, tiled roof, and a 150-foot campanile. Financial troubles nearly scuttled the campanile, but the architect persisted, and the station was dedicated on February 14, 1896. Its tower was crowned by a four-faced clock by Connecticut clockmaker Seth Thomas (who also designed the clock at Grand Central Station) that announced the station's 1 P.M. opening. A host of celebrities passed through Union Station in the heyday of rail travel, including African explorer Henry Stanley. Notable unknowns, including F. T. Matthias, also made an appearance. Matthias was an Army colonel on a top-secret mission; he boarded a train to Los Angeles on February 3, 1945, lugging a wooden box containing 100 grams of weapons-grade plutonium, which five months later ushered in the nuclear age with a mushroom cloud over the Trinity site in Los Alamos, New Mexico.

The nearly completed Union Station (minus its yet-to-be-built Italianate clock tower) is inundated by the surging Willamette during the cataclysmic flood of June 1894.

*Left:* The railroad advertised its services in newspapers—this advertisement is from 1888. *Above:* A porter conveys a load of luggage at Union Station around the turn of the century.

Pictured here is the present-day waiting room at Union Station. Architect Pietro Belluschi presided over a renovation of Union Station that lasted from 1927 to 1930. He removed cast-iron columns and added his signature Italian marble to the floors and walls of the previously unadorned waiting room.

Union Station's most distinctive feature is its 150-foot-tall clock tower. Modeled after Union Passenger Station in Worcester, Massachusetts, it was nearly abandoned due to cost overruns that plagued the station during its construction in the late 1890s. The "Go by Train" neon sign atop the clock face dates from 1948.

Amtrak's Chicago-bound Empire Builder (which has been calling on Portland since 1929) arrives at Union Station. The long, covered passenger platforms were built in anticipation of the throngs of long-distance travelers who were expected to descend upon the city for the 1905 Lewis and Clark Centennial Exposition at nearby Guild's Lake.

In 1956, Blitz Weinhard Brewing Company celebrated its 100th anniversary with bunting on the façade of the brewery's headquarters at Northwest 11th Avenue and West Burnside, when the area was known as the Industrial Triangle, a destination only for warehouse and factory workers. The red-brick brewhouse at the corner of Northwest 12th (visible behind the middle "One Way" sign), was shuttered in 1999 after the Stroh Brewing Company sold the Weinhard brand to Miller Brewing Company.

# THE PEARL DISTRICT

Henry Weinhard, Portland's king of beer, built a nine-story brewhouse on the corner of 12th and B in 1865, a year after captains Couch and Flanders opened the Gulley & Condon at Front and B. An endless supply of kegs were sent to the mariners' pub at Skid Road's end, using Couch's dock to export the company's signature lager to markets in the Orient and beyond. By the turn of the century, Weinhard's 12th Street brewhouse produced more than 100,000 barrels of beer a year, earning recognition as one of the largest—and certainly one of the oldest—breweries west of Milwaukee. After Weinhard died in 1904, his family memorialized him the only way it knew how: with a monolithic red-brick brewhouse designed by Whidden & Lewis, the architects of Portland's City Hall.

For decades, Weinhard's brewery (which dates to 1856) dominated the Northwest Industrial Triangle, a gritty district of warehouses and cobblestoned streets crisscrossed with railroad track. The area strectched from the freight yards above Union Station to the east, bordered by Skid Road in the south, with a hypotenuse of a freeway that began shunting automobile traffic onto the newly completed Fremont Bridge in 1973. In 1999, the Miller Brewing Company purchased Weinhard's and promptly closed the plant, diverting production to other breweries across the United States. A year later, Gerding Edlen, a local development firm, acquired the Weinhard complex, and the Brewery Blocks became the catalyst of one of the nation's most-lauded urban renewal projects. Over the course of a decade, Gerding Edlen transformed the gritty Industrial Triangle into an upscale enclave known as the Pearl District, converting crumbling old warehouses into gleaming loft condominiums for empty-nesters and corporate headquarters for the likes of ad giant Wieden+Kennedy. The city's fortresslike firetrap of an Armory (which Weinhard's had used as a warehouse and bottling plant) was resurrected as Portland Center Stage's Gerding Theater at the Armory. And the 1908 memorial brewhouse became the home of Henry's 12th Street Tavern in 2006. It is a 14,500-square-foot homage to the patron saint of Portland brewing—a theme park of a restaurant where Henry Weinhard's Private Reserve, which is trucked in from a Miller contractor in Hood River, is only one of the 100 beers available on tap.

## The Brewery Blocks

The Brewery Blocks are shown here under construction in July 2002 *(above)*. The nearly completed Cellar House office tower that dominates the repurposed Weinhard brewery complex (officially known as Block Two), serves as a seismic anchor for the 1908 red-brick brewhouse, which reopened as a beer-themed restaurant, Henry's 12th Street Tavern. The M Financial Building (Block Four) is shown in the photo at left while under construction—it was completed in May 2003. The construction trailers in the foreground at Block Five occupy the site of the Louisa (named for the brewmaster's wife, Louisa Weinhard), a 16-story apartment building completed in April 2005. The building has an ecoroof terrace and a parking garage with lockers for use by 100 bicycle commuters. Across from the brewhouse at Whole Foods Market (Block One), elements of the demolished Chevrolet dealership's art deco façade were incorporated into the design of the Pearl District's first grocery store, which opened in March 2002 *(above right)*. The scrim on the upper floors of the store conceals a rooftop cistern containing 12,000 tons of water. It cools the entire five-block development and is one of the many green-oriented features that earned every building in the Brewery Blocks a Leadership in Energy and Environmental Design (LEED) rating from the U.S. Green Building Council.

## BRAD CLOEPFIL

**If architect Pietro Belluschi has an heir apparent,** it's Brad Cloepfil. The wunderkind who founded his Allied Works firm in 1994 first started turning heads with shoestring designs of local restaurants—first Saucebox on Broadway in 1995, then the Pearl District's Bluehour in 2000. These were spaces that attracted the attention of ad giant Wieden+Kennedy's Dan Wieden, who commissioned the unknown maverick to transform a cold-storage warehouse into the agency's award-winning Pearl District corporate headquarters (the interior of which is pictured below). Like Belluschi's Equitable Building, international acclaim over the W+K Building led to a controversial New York City skyscraper: the Columbus Circle Lollipop Building. After the Lollipop Building, Cloepfil went on to design the St. Louis Contemporary Art Museum, the Denver Clyfford Still Museum, the Seattle Art Museum, and showcase homes before returning to his Portland hometown to redesign a new campus for the Pacific Northwest College of Art, formerly the Museum School, where Pietro Belluschi learned to draw in the 1930s.

### *Natural Capital Center*

In September 2001, Ecotrust, a Portland-based sustainability think tank, unveiled the Natural Capital Center, a warehouse dating from 1895 that was recycled into a nexus for local green-minded businesses, nonprofits, and government agencies. They range from the city's Office of Sustainable Development headquarters to a local pizzeria that funnels exhaust from its ovens into a heat exchanger, eliminating the need for a hot-water heater. The center also incorporates green features: a parking lot paved with water-permeable asphalt and bioswales that filter oil-tainted stormwater runoff. It is the first privately owned building in Oregon with bathrooms with no-water urinals, which saves 160,000 gallons of water annually.

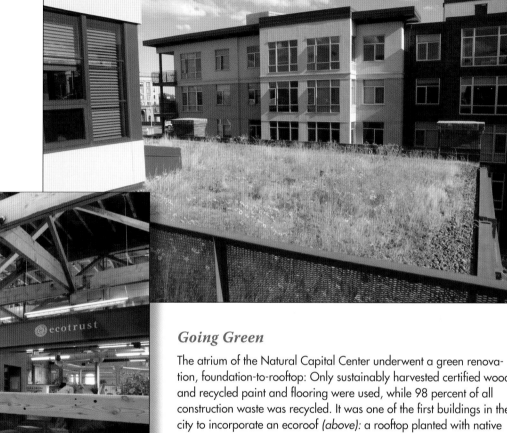

## Going Green

The atrium of the Natural Capital Center underwent a green renovation, foundation-to-rooftop: Only sustainably harvested certified wood and recycled paint and flooring were used, while 98 percent of all construction waste was recycled. It was one of the first buildings in the city to incorporate an ecoroof *(above):* a rooftop planted with native grasses and wildflowers to reduce stormwater runoff. As the first building in the Pacific Northwest to receive the U.S. Green Building Council's Gold LEED rating, the Natural Capital Center is widely credited with launching Portland's much vaunted (and imitated) green-building movement.

## Jamison Square

Jamison Square is the Pearl District's first public park, named for Pearl District pioneer William Jamison, a gallery owner who launched the initial First Thursday gallery tour in the 1990s that made the Pearl a destination. It is surrounded on all sides by high-rise loft condominium towers that once characterized the newly minted neighborhood. In June 2002, when the city first turned on the red-granite waterfall that forms a wading pool at the center of the park *(right)*, the squeals and laughter of hundreds of children could be heard, an anomaly considering that only a small percentage of the residents of the Pearl were under the age of ten. Jamison Square, much to the chagrin of some (and delight of many) of the Pearl's empty nesters, is now known as the city's foremost urban swimming hole. As then-mayor Vera Katz put it at the park's dedication, "This has been a long-anticipated day... We know that parks are very much needed here and from the day we broke ground on this site, residents have been eagerly waiting for the day the fences came down and the fountain was turned on. And it looks as if the park is a hit!"

## LOVEJOY COLUMNS

IN THE LATE 1940S, Tom Stefopoulos, a night watchman from the nearby Spokane Portland & Seattle railyard, began whiling away predawn doldrums by decorating the concrete columns—first with chalk, then with paint—of the Lovejoy Street viaduct just north of Union Station. Protected from the weather, Stefopoulos's work—doves and classical Greek figures entwined with calligraphic spiritual messages—was preserved for five decades. It achieved cult status, especially after the columns starred as the backdrop in the opening scene of Portland filmmaker Gus Van Sant's 1989 *Drugstore Cowboy*. Around the time the film debuted, the former Northwest Industrial Triangle began its rapid evolution into the Pearl District, which led the city to tear down the viaduct in 1999. Fans of Stefopoulos (and Van Sant) lobbied the city to preserve the columns; two of them found a new home in the courtyard of the Elizabeth Lofts condominium development at Northwest 10th and Flanders.

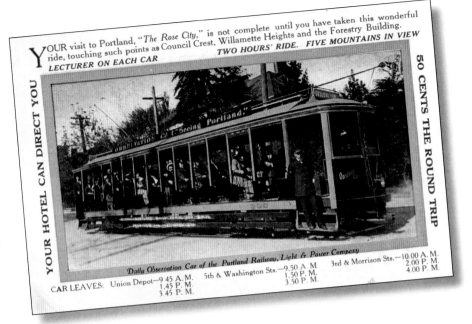

*Above:* This undated postcard advertises a tourist trolley run by the Portland Railway, Light and Power Company (which in 1928 operated trolleys on 200 miles of track) that circumnavigated the city, from Union Station (then called Union Depot) to Council Crest and the Forestry Building at Guild's Lake.

Shown here are three of the graffiti-covered concrete columns supporting the now-demolished Lovejoy Street Viaduct, photographed in May 1954, not long after they were painted by railyard worker Tom Stefopolous.

*Right:* Designed by New York City sculptor Kenny Scharf (a contemporary of the late graffiti artist Keith Haring), the colorful totem poles found around the perimeter of Jamison Square are actually a clever disguise: They conceal catenary poles supporting the wires that power the Pearl's equally colorful peoplemover. The "Go by Streetcar" neon sign on the façade of the Streetcar Lofts condominium tower mimics the postwar signage on Union Station's campanile.

# NOB HILL

Before John Heard Couch died in 1870, he subdivided the undeveloped land on the family claim's upper quadrant into a residential area, reserving a double block along Northwest 19th Street for each of his four daughters and his brother-in-law and business partner, George Flanders. From 1881 to 1885, all but his youngest daughter, Mary Couch, who moved to Paris, had built lavish three-story mansions on Northwest 19th and subdivided the neighborhood beyond, which became known variously as Nob Hill, the Alphabet District, and the West End. Until streetcars opened the Tualatin Mountains for development at the turn of the century, Nob Hill, and particularly Northwest 19th, was one of the city's most enviable enclaves. Although the Couch family mansions were razed long ago to make room for apartment houses and other "improvements," a few family artifacts remain, most notably the Victorian at 2063 Northwest Hoyt, a schoolhouse Couch's wife, Caroline, built in 1884 for the clan's 15 grandchildren.

In the late 20th century, Northwest 23rd superseded Northwest 19th as the neighborhood's noted avenue. Along the commercial strip that some deride as "Northwest Trendythird"—from the outskirts of the industrial district on Vaughan to Couch's namesake street—brewpubs, boutiques, restaurants, and cafes do business in painted Victorians, some of questionable heritage. For example, the historic Pettygrove House, a Victorian on the corner of Northwest 23rd and Pettygrove with a coffeehouse serving raspberry crepes and mugs of Stumptown, is often described as the former home of Portland founder Francis Pettygrove. Never mind that the house was built in 1892, five years after Pettygrove's death. Or 41 years after he sold his stake in Portland and relocated to Washington, where he cofounded the already-named city of Port Townsend.

Image cropped

The four homes pictured here were built by relatives of Captain John Heard Couch between 1881 and 1885, including (from far left to right) brother-in-law George Flanders, daughter Clementine (the home with the cupola), granddaughter Mary Caroline Wilson (foreground), and just visible behind Wilson's home, the home of Couch's eldest daughter, Caroline.

The Willamette Heights trolley, shown here circa 1904, ran along Nob Hill's 23rd Street, ending at the entrance of City Park. It made its final run on February 26, 1950.

Along Northwest 21st and 23rd avenues in present-day Nob Hill, former single-family Georgian and Victorian homes are now occupied by coffee shops, restaurants, and boutiques.

In 1884, John Heard Couch's widow, Caroline, built a Nob Hill home for use as a schoolhouse. In 1914, two years before the building was carted away and used once again as a home, the Couch School relocated to a much larger campus on Northwest Glisan Street that was designed by architect Floyd A. Naramore (the chief architect of public school districts in Portland and Seattle), and served as an elementary school for Nob Hill children. Although the ornately carved crest over the school's main entrance still bears the initials CES (for Couch Elementary School), children enrolled there today know it only by its generic new name: the Metropolitan Learning Center.

# GUILD'S LAKE

This photo shows the view looking east toward the Willamette River from the Tualatin Mountains (known today as the West Hills) in June 1903, two years before New York City landscape architect John Charles Olmsted transformed Guild's Lake—a shallow tidal marsh where the city dumped its garbage—into the Venice-like fairgrounds of the Lewis and Clark Centennial Exposition.

John Charles Olmsted proved his genius as a landscape architect when he transformed Guild's Lake (named after the claim's original settlers, who pronounced their name as "Guiled")—a 598-acre tract dominated by a tidal lake and the city's primary garbage dump—into the exquisitely sculpted fairgrounds of the Lewis and Clark Centennial Exposition. But soon after the fair ended (fall 1905), the fairgrounds were sold to developers. Lafeyette Pence, a former Colorado legislator turned shady land speculator, focused his efforts on Guild's Lake. Without bothering to ask the city for permission, Pence began blasting the hillside above the lake. He started with dynamite, then used a water cannon fed by an elaborate flume system that diverted Balch Creek. In the process, the entrance to Macleay Park was destroyed. Pence was determined to fill Guild's Lake at any cost and vowed to level the Tualatin Mountains until Mayor Harry Lane famously took a sledgehammer to Pence's illegal sluiceworks. After Pence disappeared—having filled in a portion of the lake with 220,000 cubic yards of silt—another company with proper permits terraced the hillside for a housing development, the present-day Westover Terrace. In the 1920s, the city finished the job that Pence had started, filling the lake with more than 20 million cubic yards of silt dredged from the Willamette River. During World War II, the area became Guild's Lake Court, a temporary home for 10,000 shipyard workers. Factories and warehouses followed. All that remains of John Olmsted's fairgrounds is the area's all-but-unknown official name: The Guild's Lake Industrial Sanctuary.

During the summer of 1905, fairgoers descended a staircase leading to the Bridge of the Nations, a span over Guild's Lake to the U.S. Government Building.

Lewis & Clark Exposition
Portland Oregon

DAYTON, OHIO — NATIONAL CASH REGISTER
A TRIP TO THE N.C.R. MOTION PICTURES · FREE ·

### The Cash Register Building

Fairgoers at the 1905 Lewis and Clark Centennial Exposition mingle outside the National Cash Register Company's exhibition hall *(left)*, which featured a short silent film—a novelty at the time. After the fair ended, the company donated the building to the First Congregational Church of St. Johns. The building was barged across the river and pulled up the hill using a team of horses to its present location on North Richmond Street, where it still draws crowds as a pub and movie theater *(below)*.

### GUILD'S LAKE BUILDINGS

**THE PORTLAND PARK BOARD** considered preserving the Guild's Lake fairgrounds as Lewis and Clark Memorial Park but ultimately concluded in a 1903 report that "it is to be regretted that the ground is almost entirely leased territory and that most of the improvements will either disappear or revert to private use." Which is exactly what happened. After the fair ended in the fall of 1905, some of the spectacular exhibition halls—such as the U.S. Government Building—fell into ruins. Others were carted away. The Massachusetts Building, a hand-me-down from the 1904 St. Louis World's Fair, was reincarnated as the Crystal Springs Sanitarium on the slopes of southeast Portland's Mount Tabor. In 1910, the building became Josselyn Hall, the residence of Bennage Josselyn, the president of Portland Railway, Light and Power Company. The National Cash Register Company's onion-domed exhibition hall, reassembled in St. Johns, served as a funeral parlor and bingo hall before the McMenamin brothers purchased it in 1998 and turned it into the St. Johns Pub. Only one building, the Forestry Building, remained on the site; too big to move, it served as a public museum until it also disappeared, consumed by a raging fire in 1964.

# FOREST PARK

By the turn of the century, just about all of the land between the Willamette River and the Tualatin Mountains had been divided and subdivided and developed. The eight-mile stretch of the mountains that dominated the horizon beyond Couch's Addition from the summit of B Street north to Sauvie Island, however, remained uninhabited—the forested slopes deemed too steep and prone to slides to be suitable for development. In 1899, a minister named Thomas Lamb Eliot urged the city to establish a parks commission to explore the prospects of convincing other property owners to follow the example of real estate magnate Donald Macleay. Macleay had donated a 108-acre tract along Balch Creek because he didn't want to pay taxes on land he couldn't develop. If more land was given up, the entire northern flank of the mountains could be conserved as a public preserve, called Forest Park. In the spring of 1903, the city's new Park Board hired John C. Olmsted (the nephew and adopted son of Central Park designer Frederick Law Olmsted) to visit Portland and assess the city's greenspaces—foremost, the prospects of fledgling Forest Park.

Olmsted's jaw dropped when he saw what he described in his report as "a succession of ravines and spurs covered with remarkably beautiful primeval woods." Olmsted urged the city to acquire the acreage, predicting that "future generations will...bless the men who were wise enough to get such woods preserved."

But Forest Park remained unrealized until another esteemed New York City urban planner, Robert Moses, visited Portland 40 years later—at the behest of city planners—and issued another report, scolding Portlanders for failing to act on Forest Park. "The city has not taken full advantage of its great natural assets," Moses wrote, urging that "the steep wooded hillsides located on the westerly border of the City be placed in public ownership...[and] are as important to Portland as the Palisades of the Hudson are to New York City."

Chagrined, Portlanders finally rallied around Forest Park. Property was seized from delinquent taxpayers, including 1,400 acres from hundreds of investors who had purchased lots in an ill-conceived subdivision, platted along a road that washed away the year it was completed. Donations from landowners were also consolidated. Finally, the city dedicated Forest Park on September 28, 1948. Today, stretching eight miles and encompassing 5,000 wooded acres with 30 miles of trails, it's the largest urban preserve in America.

It took from 1905 to 1914 for *The Oregonian* publisher Henry Pittock to finish Pittock Mansion (pictured above), a 22-room French Renaissance chateau off West Burnside Street, now a city-owned museum that's a popular destination for Forest Park hikers and picnickers.

Shown here is a domed foyer leading to one of Pittock Mansion's many balconies. As *TIME* magazine noted in a 1938 profile, on the night before his death, Pittock "had himself carried to the east bay of his grey stone mansion on Portland's Imperial Heights, to look once more across the city where he had made his fortune." Undoubtedly, he also wanted to see the summit of Mount Hood, where he had ascended to the top of Oregon in 1857.

One of the most popular landmarks along Forest Park's 30-mile-long Wildwood Trail is the Stone House, a wilderness way station and bathroom that Depression-era laborers built in 1929. After the Columbus Day Storm of 1962 (a typhoon that brought winds of up to 116 mph to downtown Portland) knocked out the facility's water line, vandals so thoroughly finished the demolition job started by the typhoon that the Portland parks department decided to strip the building down to its stonework rather than rebuild it.

## BALCH CREEK

BALCH CREEK IS A BUCOLIC stream that begins up in the West Hills and tumbles through Forest Park's Macleay Park before disappearing into a culvert that carries it beneath the industrial park that used to be Guild's Lake. The creek was named for Danford Balch, the first person to be legally hanged in the city of Portland. Balch, a pioneer who came to Portland with his wife in 1850, established a farm on a 350-acre tract that cuts through the present-day park and the neighborhood of Willamette Heights. In 1858, Balch hired a farmhand named Mortimer Stump, who fell in love with Balch's 16-year-old daughter, Anna, and asked for her hand. When Balch refused, the couple eloped to Vancouver, Washington. Two weeks later, shotgun in hand, Balch followed the newlyweds to Jimmy Stephens's Willamette River ferry and confronted Stump, intending to bring his daughter home. In the ensuing scuffle, Balch shot Stump, killing him instantly. At his trial, Balch professed his innocence, claiming that the gun had been triggered accidentally. Nonetheless, the court found Balch guilty and sentenced him to death. A gallows was erected on Front Street and Salmon in October 1859, and two weeks before Halloween, a crowd of more than 500—including Anna Balch—gathered to witness the hanging.

In 1921, city engineers diverted Balch Creek into a sewer pipe that carried the creek underground from its exit at Forest Park's Macleay Park, beneath Guild's Lake (pictured in the background), and into the Willamette.

# THE SWITZERLAND OF AMERICA

The Tualatin Mountains of Southwest Portland rise from sea level to an altitude of slightly more than a thousand feet, but to the first settlers, they must have seemed as imposing as the Alps, forming a natural barrier that confined the city's westward expansion. Portland's first great triumph, an event that some say sealed its rise as the state's dominant metropolis, was heralded in the Park Blocks near the present-day Portland Art Museum.

A ceremony dedicated the opening of the Great Plank Road, a highway of rough-hewn cedar planks that crested today's West Hills and connected Portland with the Tualatin Plains, giving farmers in the Willamette Valley a direct link to the wharves of Captain Couch and a market to the world beyond.

## COUNCIL CREST

Aside from the first bridge that spanned the Willamette in 1887, arguably the next great engineering milestone was the Portland Cable Railway, a short-lived cable car system modeled after San Francisco's that opened the West Hills to development in 1890. As the downtown commercial district expanded, more and more homes were demolished to make room for office buildings and storefronts until the only place left to settle on the west side of the Willamette was the previously inaccessible hills above the city. On February 22, the Portland Cable Railway began shuttling commuters up a 1,004-foot-long wooden trestle with a 21 percent grade to Portland Heights, a picnic spot that soon became the city's most prestigious address and attracted luminaries. Poet C.E.S. Wood built a luxurious mansion on present-day Southwest Vista Avenue that Portland grand dame Barbara Bartlett Hartwell described as "the most romantic house in Portland." Many others followed.

This is a bird's-eye view of Portland from an unidentified location in the West Hills taken on August 6, 1908. A brochure promoting the view of downtown Portland from the Council Crest neighborhood declared, "The great white chiefs, the Captains of Industry, those who will not be the toilers, but the sages of all sages, will say unto themselves: 'Here, too, will I erect my teepee in wood, brick, concrete and stone.'"

*Left:* The lights of downtown Portland can be seen from the West Hills, shown here in May 1987. At sundown in 1898, leading a carriage-load of visiting clerics to the city from a promontory they named Council Crest, publisher George Himes wrote, "The electric lights over the whole city were revealed... a patch of starlight had been taken from the heavens and turned upside down."

By 1904, an electric trolley line extended the reach to the highest point in Portland: Council Crest. The city park owes its name to Portland publisher George Himes, who, in July 1898, conveyed six carriageloads of visiting clerics from the Council of Congregational churches to the then-anonymous promontory at sundown and asked them for a name. "The group chose Council Crest because its representatives came to the city at our feet for mutual council," wrote Himes.

"The party descended to the city by a circuitous route of several miles. With one accord the entire company were enthusiastic over the wonderful scenic surroundings of the city, claiming that it could not be matched in all its striking diversity anywhere upon this earth of ours."

The observation wasn't lost on developers after the opening of the Council Crest trolley line. In a 1908 sales brochure, H. W. Lemcke Company invented an alternate but more romantic backstory to lure homebuyers to the neighborhood, purporting in "History of Council Crest Park" that Chief Multnomah favored the site as place to conduct councils of war.

## NEIGHBORHOOD SELLING POINTS

Another firm marketed nearby Healy Heights as "The Switzerland of America" in a beautifully gilded 1912 book with letterpress type and hand-painted illustrations. It recounted the wanderings of a Tyrolean prince, who at the end of the day, made his bed in Healy Heights, where "All about him the artist feels a sense of perfect security and contentment."

The Council Crest line disappeared in 1950 with the advent of the diesel bus, but in 2007, replicas of the trolleys began trundling along freshly laid tracks in Southwest Portland's hottest new real estate venture—South Waterfront, an industrial wasteland at the foot of Marquam Hill reborn as a luxury riverfront condominium community. In 2006, reviving the notion of the Southwest Hills as the Switzerland of America, a 3,300-foot-long aerial tramway began whisking residents up Marquam Hill to Oregon Health & Science University, the city's largest employer. The pill-shape stainless steel gondolas were built in Bern, and the tramway—perhaps not coincidentally—is operated by Doppelmayer, the Swiss ski lift company that runs the Matterhorn Express.

In 1890, three years after the Morrison Bridge became the first span across the Willamette, the Portland Cable Railway Company built a thousand-foot-long trestle to the summit of the Tualatin Mountains (a.k.a. the West Hills). After leaving the entrance of City Park, the cable line continued along Southwest Jefferson Street, then turned onto Southwest 18th Avenue and climbed the trestle, which began near the avenue's intersection with present-day Sunset Highway. It topped out at present-day Southwest Clifton Street, bridging the way to residential development of Portland's previously inaccessible highlands and giving birth to an upper-crust neighborhood known as Portland Heights. Despite spectacular mishaps involving runaway trains, cable cars continued to climb the trestle to Portland Heights until 1904, when electric trolleys began rolling over the newly completed Ford Street Bridge span (the precursor of present-day Vista Bridge) over Canyon Road, consigning Portland's cable railway, and its troublesome trestle, to history.

Observation Car of the Portland Railway, Light and Power Co., Portland, Oregon

This picture postcard from 1909 depicts a Portland Railway, Light and Power Company sightseeing car making the climb to Council Crest. The company was a privately owned public transportation colossus formed in 1906, when Portland Railway merged with Oregon Water Power & Railway and Portland General Electric Company.

Cementing the notion of the West Hills as "The Switzerland of America," the City of Portland hired a team of Swiss ski lift engineers to build the Portland Aerial Tram in 2005, which began ferrying passengers from the South Waterfront neighborhood to the summit of Marquam Hill in December 2006.

In this lithograph from the 1880s, Tanner Creek follows Canyon Road as it winds down from the hills in the foreground. At the bottom of the hill, Tanner Creek loops around the neighborhood of Goose Hollow, then makes another 180-degree bend around Daniel Lownsdale's tannery (the future home of Multnomah Field, now PGE Park). It crosses under B Avenue (present-day Burnside) and ambles through Couch's Addition and Couch Lake before emptying into the Willamette. In 1886, a 500-foot portion of the creek at the bottom of the hill was channeled into a brick sewer pipe, which ultimately extended all the way to the river.

# GOOSE HOLLOW

This Tualatin Mountains foothills neighborhood derives its name from a legal dispute that arose over the geese that ran wild here during the 1860s. Property owners couldn't tell whose goose was whose, so the neighbors took the matter to court, and a judge ordered the flock to be split equally among the residents. *The Oregonian* dubbed it "The Goose Hollow War," prompting the area to be called Goose Hollow.

The "Hollow" referred to the area's then most prominent feature: a deep gulch created by Tanner Creek, which cut through the heart of present-day Goose Hollow. Chinese farmers cultivated vegetables along its banks until the turn of the century. The creek was named after a tannery—the first on the west coast—that Daniel Lownsdale (the pioneer who once owned the tract, purchased from founder Francis Pettygrove) established in

1845 on the banks of the creek near the place where it crossed under B Street. It's said that the vats Lownsdale fashioned from creek-bed basalt remain beneath the stadium (present-day PGE Park) that was built atop the tannery in 1893.

Today, light rail tracks emerging from Robertson Tunnel at the foot of the mountain follow the path of the former creek bed, which was

channeled into a sewer pipe in the late 1800s. At the Goose Hollow station, beside a waist-high bronze goose, a stone marker set into the platform traces the creek's path, etched with the inscription: "In the eons before the city, a creek flowed right where you are standing…now it winds below the city hidden forty feet beneath this very spot." You can hear it calling from a nearby sewer grate, murmuring in its cavern underground.

In the lowlands of Goose Hollow, Chinese farmers erected shacks along the banks of Tanner Creek, pictured here in the early 1890s. They stood in stark contrast to the mansions on the double lots of King's Hill, a subdivision real estate developer Amos King built near the entrance of Portland's new City Park.

This view of the Goose Hollow neighborhood was photographed during the winter of 1949, from the Vista Bridge, looking east along Southwest Jefferson Avenue.

In this 1965 photo, Portland City Council members pose for a photograph on the steps of the Jacob Kamm House, an 1872 Goose Hollow mansion rescued from demolition.

## PGE Park

After a major renovation in 2001, Portland General Electric Company bought the naming rights to Civic Stadium, which became known as PGE Park. Early in 2009, Merritt Paulson, the owner of the Portland Timbers and the Portland Beavers, announced plans for an $85 million upgrade of the stadium, this time to accommodate the city's first Major League Soccer franchise, expected in 2011. The eight-foot-tall bronze mask outside the stadium's main entrance is one of pair of sculptures at either end of the plaza titled *Facing the Crowd,* installed in 2001 by San Diego sculptor Michael Stutz.

From right to left: Oregon Governor Walter M. Pierce, President Warren G. Harding, First Lady Florence Harding, Portland Mayor George Baker, F. E. Andrews (Chamber of Commerce president), and U.S. Secretary of Commerce Herbert Hoover review the crowd gathered at the First Baptist Church on the corner of Southwest 12th Avenue and Taylor during Harding's visit to the city in July 1923. More than 30,000 Portlanders came to Multnomah Field (the future PGE Park) on July 4 that year to hear the President deliver one of the last speeches of his life.

Soccer fans pack PGE Park, home turf of the minor league Portland Timbers, to watch an international match between Australia and Ghana at the FIFA Women's World Cup on September 28, 2003.

The Portland Beavers trace their history to 1903, when the team began play as the Portland Baseball Club at Vaughan Street Park in Northwest Portland; they became the Beavers in 1906. After Vaughan Street Park was bulldozed in 1955, the team moved to Civic Stadium. When the Beavers moved to Spokane in 1972, actor Kurt Russell played a season at the stadium for a minor league team called the Mavericks that filled in for the Beavers until the team's return in 1978. Here, catcher Quintero Humberto (left) greets his teammates after being introduced to the crowd at the home opener against the Las Vegas 51s on April 16, 2004.

Portland's soon-to-be major league soccer team, the Timbers, attracts a boisterous following of fans calling themselves the Timbers Army. Seated in the stadium's north end, known as the Woodshed, the Timbers Army, shown here during an exhibition game on July 23, 2005, cheers an emissary of the Black Cats of Sunderland, England. The green and yellow banner hoisted by fans refers to the team's mascot, Jim Serrill, a.k.a. "Timber Jim," a professional lumberjack who retired in 2008. His successor, "Timber Joe," carries on the Timbers Army tradition of celebrating each home team goal by firing up his Stihl and carving up a log.

# WASHINGTON PARK

In 1871, in a distant corner of the hills just above Goose Hollow, a developer named Amos King sold the city a little over 40 acres of woodland at the west end of Jefferson Street for $32,624 (more than half a million dollars today). When King (who had purchased Daniel Lownsdale's tannery and holdings in 1852) began selling off double lots at the foot of the mountainous timberland (the present-day King's Hill neighborhood), many complained that the city had been conned into buying a worthless piece of real estate: an impenetrable forest at the head of a steep canyon a mile west of downtown that was all but inaccessible to the public. Still, the city persevered and hired a groundskeeper, Charles M. Meyers, who erected a greenhouse and began sculpting a series of formal gardens modeled after the parks he had frequented as a boy in Germany. In January 1890, a San Francisco–style cable car began servicing the park (and King's subdivision). The bickering ended, and Portlanders embraced City Park as Portland's equivalent of Central Park.

John Olmsted was impressed when he surveyed the city's parks in 1903, and his report to the Park Board included a few suggestions for improving City Park. Foremost, Olmsted recommended relocating the entrance to a more accessible street, expanding it considerably. He also suggested changing its name because "the name of the existing park is not distinctive enough ... 'Pioneer Park' would be a more euphonious title, but might be thought to be imitating Seattle."

The Park Board took Olmsted to heart, changing City Park's name to Washington Park and relocating the main entrance to Southwest Park Place in 1904. In 1917, an International Rose Test Garden was built on a six-acre landslide that had been abandoned by developers in 1894. Five years later, the city annexed the County Poor Farm, which occupied 160 acres just up the canyon from the old park entrance, converting the grounds into an arboretum and golf course. The space ultimately became the home of the city's zoo in 1959 and has been joined by other attractions over the years, including the Portland Children's Museum and the World Forestry Center.

In 1891, the city paid Swiss sculptor Hans Staehli to cast the *Chiming Fountain,* the first public artwork commissioned for City Park (renamed Washington Park). *Chiming Fountain,* named for the sound the water makes as it cascades from one basin to the next, sits in a circle just above the main entrance. The cherub that once adorned the upper bowl disappeared a decade after this photo was taken in 1902.

## TYRRELL TRIPS
### SEEING PORTLAND AUTOMOBILES

Leave Stand 10 A. M., 2 P. M., 4 P. M.

By no means fail to take our delightful sunset and foothill trip, passing from the thickly populated districts, through suburban drives and sections of fragrant foliage and on to primitive life in the foothills, concluding with a moonlight ride through Chinatown, showing the quaint and peculiar habits of the Chinese. The lecturer will treat of early-day history on the old Oregon country. An 18-mile ride. Fare, $1.00. Car leaves stand, Fourth and Washington, at 6:30 P. M.

Make your reservations early.

PHONES EXCHANGE 11   A 6171

I WAS IN PORTLAND AND TOOK THIS TRIP

This 1908 picture postcard of a jitney laden with sightseers near the West Burnside entrance of Washington Park *(above)* was distributed as a souvenir of—and advertisement for, as shown in the accompanying text *(left)*—a popular tourist excursion through downtown Portland and beyond.

### WASHINGTON PARK STATION

AT 260 FEET BELOW GROUND, Washington Park's light rail station is the deepest transit stop in North America and is the second deepest in the world after Moscow's Park Pobedy. The station sits in the center of the Robertson Tunnel, which is made up of twin 3.1-mile-long shafts that were punched through the bowels of the Tualatin Mountains in the 1990s, connecting downtown with the suburbs of Beaverton and Hillsboro. Digging the tunnels cost nearly a billion dollars and took almost three years. Workers began dynamiting the westbound tunnel entrance at the foot of the mountain in Goose Hollow in the summer of 1993, while on the opposite side of the mountain, a 500-ton excavator called Bore-Regard began chewing through basalt at a rate of 15 feet per day in August 1994; the crews met in the middle 16 months later. The workers were quick learners—they dug the other tunnel in only four months.

## Grace and Brownie

In 1888, pharmacist Richard M. Knight, who kept a menagerie next door to his drugstore on Morrison Street, donated the first animals in the city zoo—a grizzly named Grace and a brown bear named Brownie. This illustration of Grace and Brownie in the zoo's new bear pit in City Park was published in *West Shore* magazine in May 1890.

A wooden water tank resembling a Dutch windmill towers over one of the animal houses at the city zoo in 1900. John C. Olmsted approved of the zoo's spartan aesthetics. "Every dollar of available park funds would much better be expended in the acquisition of lands, and for the long but economical drives and walks needed to make them available," he noted in his 1903 report to the Park Board.

By 1925, encroaching residential development forced the zoo to relocate to a more remote area between the present-day Japanese Gardens and the Sherwood Meadows archery range before moving one last time, in 1959, to a golf course that had been built on the grounds of the former County Poor Farm. The number of Portlanders passing through the zoo's gates (pictured here) in 2008, spurred by the birth of a baby elephant, topped 1.5 million, making the Oregon Zoo the state's most visited attraction.

At 5:58 A.M. on April 14, 1962, an Asian elephant named Belle gave birth to a 225-pound baby. Christened Packy—the name had been decided by a city council vote—it was the first pachyderm (thick-skinned mammals including the elephant, rhinoceros, and hippopotamus) born in captivity in the Western Hemisphere in more than four decades and only the sixth elephant born in America since 1796. Packy heralded a wave of elephant births in Oregon, beginning six months later with Me-Tu, followed by 27 others over the next four decades. The birth of Samudra on August 22, 2008, inspired voters to pass a $125 million Oregon Zoo bond measure that included $30 million for the zoo's elephants.

## *International Rose Test Garden*

In 1917, as war raged in Europe, members of Portland's Rose Society (founded by Georgiana Pittock in 1888) voted to establish an International Rose Test Garden to serve as a sanctuary for rare hybrids sent from gardens in England and France that were threatened with bombardment. For the effort, the city donated a six-acre parcel of land on the northern edge of Washington Park that developers had cleared of trees and terraced for home sites in the 1890s, but had abandoned after the real estate market collapsed with the panic of 1893. The terraced slopes, affording one of the finest views of downtown and Mount Hood, proved idyllic, and the garden, shown here present-day, thrived. More than 7,000 varieties blossom every June, heralding the onset of the city's annual Rose Festival.

## Japanese Garden

Four years after the Oregon Zoo vacated the hillside above Washington Park's rose garden in 1959, a group of Portland citizens calling themselves the Japanese Garden Society of Oregon hired Takuma Tono, the head of the landscape architecture program at the University of Tokyo, to draw up plans for a formal Japanese garden and supervise construction. Tono divided the Portland Japanese Garden, which opened in 1967, into five distinct gardens: a Strolling Pond Garden where the "Heavenly Falls" churn a koi pond that flows beneath a Moon Bridge (pictured); a Tea Garden, with a formal tea house that was built in Japan and shipped to Oregon in pieces; a Natural Garden where the greenery is left to grow wild; a flat garden where sand imported from Japan's Shirakawa River is raked around islands shaped like a sake gourd and cup, signifying hospitality; and a Sand and Stone Garden, with weathered stones rising from a sea of sand raked into elaborate patterns.

## Hoyt Arboretum

In 1928, the City Council designated a 145-acre tract of the former County Poor Farm as Hoyt Arboretum, but since they were lacking funds, the first trees weren't planted until three years later. After more than 70 years of uninterrupted growth, the Arboretum's canopy—10,000 specimens representing 1,000 species—stretches unbroken, pierced only by a grove of sequoias that Stumptown's lumber-hungry pioneers likely deemed too magnificent to axe.

# MULTNOMAH VILLAGE

Multnomah Village owes its existence—and its name—to banker Henry Corbett and Charles F. Swigert (the engineer who built the city's first bridge), who teamed up with a few other investors to push the Oregon Electric Railway over the Tualatin Mountains in 1907. Before Oregon Electric, the city's first commuter railroad (connecting Portland to Oregon's capital city, Salem, and Eugene), the community of around 40 Swiss dairy farms was called "Home Addition." The moniker wouldn't do for a railroad station, so Oregon Electric changed it to the romantic-sounding "Multnomah," after a legendary Indian chief. Interurban service brought land speculators, then homebuyers who became commuters, and soon, a Mayberry-like main street grew up around the train station. Gradually the cow pastures were subdivided into lots, and the village of Multnomah became the city's first bedroom community.

By the 1920s, as driving trumped public transit, freight trains replaced passenger trains, and eventually the trains stopped running altogether; the tracks were torn up and the depot became a grocery store, which is the present-day John's Marketplace. After the city annexed Multnomah in the 1950s, and one-stop supermarkets like Fred Meyer opened on nearby Southwest Barbur Boulevard, the area deteriorated. But the village's fortunes rose as downtown Portland's did. Entrepreneurs and artisans discovered the street and began fixing it up, and young homebuyers discovered affordable cottages where many of the dirt streets remained, and the air still smelled of the country.

### John's Marketplace

In 1907, the sleepy village of Multnomah awakened when it became a stop along the Oregon Electric Railway, Oregon's first commuter railroad. As passenger trains waned with the rise of the automobile, the rails were removed. Today, all that remains is the asphalt road that replaced the railway, Southwest Multnomah Boulevard, and John's Marketplace, a grocery store founded in 1923 by Swiss immigrant John Feus; it moved into the former depot in 1958.

*Left:* Southwest Capitol Highway turns into Main Street U.S.A. when it passes through downtown Multnomah Village; Fat City Café has been luring Portlanders from downtown—and City Hall—for breakfast and lunch since it opened in 1974. A sign that says "The Police Chief Was Fired Here" hangs at the booth where Portland Mayor Bud Clark dismissed his top cop over coffee in 1987.

### Alpenrose Dairy

Before the railroad arrived in Multnomah, the village was surrounded on all sides by clover and alfalfa fields tended by Swiss dairy farmers who settled the area in the late 1800s. In 1891, Alpenrose Dairy was founded by Florian Cadonau, a Swiss émigré who owned a small dairy near present-day Southwest Vermont Street and 35th Avenue and delivered milk in gallon cans by wagon to restaurants in downtown Portland. Over the next century, four generations of Cadonaus have evolved the business—which still provides milk and ice cream for the Portland metropolitan area—into a multivaried milk-fortified theme park. It contains a western-style frontier town, a 600-seat opera house with a Skinner pipe organ rescued from Portland's Civic Auditorium, midget car racing (races with very small, high-powered race cars), and the Alpenrose Velodrome (pictured here), one of 20 banked bicycle racetracks in the United States.

### Handy Andy Gas Station

In the 1950s, after superstore pioneer Fred Meyer opened an outlet on nearby Southwest Barbur Boulevard, Multnomah Village's shopping district deteriorated while businesses that catered to motorists (like the Handy Andy station pictured here in 1966) thrived.

# ELK ROCK GARDENS

In 1897, Scottish-born grain exporter Peter Kerr (along with one of his brothers, Thomas, and business partner Patrick Gifford) purchased a 13-acre estate three miles south of Portland called Cliff Cottage. It was perched high on a sheer basalt promontory overlooking an island in the Willamette known as Elk Rock. Over the next eight years, the three young bachelors held a succession of much-talked-about parties on their estate, which they called the "Cliff Cottage Club." Meals were catered by their Chinese cook, Chin Yin Ling, and the parties centered around champagne and croquet, tennis, and golf on the expansive lawn around the three-story Victorian. In a self-published and hand-illustrated journal titled *The Veracious Chronicles of the Cliff Cottage Club,* Kerr, who referred to himself as club president, chronicled the exploits of the bachelors—plus their two terriers Towzer and Nib; an Irish setter, Bulgar; their flock of Wyandotte chickens; and occasionally, Kerr siblings Andrew and David. They played jokes on visiting celebrities, such as the time poet C.E.S. Wood fell asleep in the parlor on a hot July afternoon only to wake up sweat-drenched in a stifling 150-degree sauna after the bachelors lit a blazing fire in the hearth.

When Peter Kerr married in 1905, he bought out his partners' shares and converted the Cliff Cottage Club into his family home. Following the birth of two daughters, Kerr asked architect D. E. Lawrence to draw up plans for a proper house, a rambling mansion modeled after the Scottish manor home he remembered from his ancestral homeland. In 1912, two years before construction started on his new home (which was completed in 1916), Kerr began sculpting an elaborate series of gardens based in part on a design devised by landscape impresario John Olmsted. Over the next decade, Kerr transformed six acres into a formal English garden resplendent with wisteria, koi ponds, waterfalls, and a vast lawn that recalls the croquet matches of the Cliff Cottage Club bachelors. After his death at age 95 in 1957, Kerr's daughters donated the manor house to the Episcopal Diocese of Oregon, which uses the home as the adminstrative headquarters of the presiding bishop. The grounds were deeded to the city of Portland as a public park, which is known as the Elk Rock Gardens of the Bishop's Close.

Image cropped

Peter (middle left) and Andrew Kerr, along with two unidentified houseguests, prepare for a mixed doubles tennis match on the grass court of their cliff-top estate on the Willamette River. From 1897 to the early 1900s, Cliff Cottage Club parties were legendary among Portland's social scene.

Pictured here is the main lawn of the Scottish-style manor house that replaced Cliff Cottage in 1916. It now serves as The Bishop's Close, the administrative offices of the Episcopal Diocese of Oregon.

### Elk Rock Gardens

When heirs of Peter Kerr donated the estate to the Episcopal Diocese of Oregon in the late 1950s, they stipulated that the six acres of manicured grounds would forever serve as a public park. Called Elk Rock Gardens, they are perched atop a cliff above the Willamette River overlooking an island known as Elk Rock.

# LAIR HILL

Named for William Lair Hill, an editor of *The Oregonian* who briefly owned property there in the 1870s, Lair Hill was one of the first areas of the city to be settled and one of Portland's most diverse neighborhoods. It boomed in 1886, when the area—a mostly flat tract stretching from the river to the mountains south of downtown—became the southern terminus of the city's first street railway.

Lair Hill attracted waves of immigrants from Eastern Europe who worked at the waterfront lumber mill. They rarely left the enclave with its close-knit commercial strip of groceries, delis, and ethnic businesses that thrived when a streetcar route was established along 1st Street. Due to the area's diversity, a few well-heeled Portlanders put up cast-iron fences to keep out the riffraff. The most notable was Charles E. Smith, the owner of an iron foundry who built a conspicuous mansion in the heart of the neighborhood at the site of present-day Lair Hill Park. Immigrant families began to leave as opportunities arose, an exodus hastened by ill-planned infrastructure projects including the Ross Island Bridge in 1926, Harbor Drive in the 1950s, and Interstate 5 in the 1960s, which fragmented the formerly cohesive neighborhood.

In 2005, wary Lair Hill residents—mostly young professionals—fought the construction of the aerial tramway. Regardless, in 2007, the tram began shuttling doctors and nurses from a new development on the neighborhood's long-decrepit waterfront to the campus of the Oregon Health & Science University at the summit of Marquam Hill. Although Lair Hill residents lost the tram battle, they did win one concession: a pedestrian and bike bridge over Interstate 5.

When this aerial view was taken around the turn of the century, Lair Hill was a working-class neighborhood and one of the most ethnically diverse enclaves in the city.

The view from atop Marquam Hill in 1958 looks north over downtown Portland and Mount Saint Helens. The homes in the foreground are typical of the Lair Hill neighborhood, which at the turn of the century attracted waves of immigrants from Eastern Europe, including a sizable Jewish community.

In 1910, the National Council of Jewish Women built Lair Hill's Neighborhood House, a Georgian Revival style home designed by noted Portland architect A. E. Doyle. It aided newly arrived Jewish immigrants, offering English classes, a clinic, a library, and a Hebrew school. In 2000, Neighborhood House became the home of the Cedarwood School, a private Waldorf elementary school.

This proposed design for the Gibbs Street Pedestrian and Bike Bridge is slated for completion in 2010. It may be the first extradosed bridge (a cross between a girder bridge and a cable-stayed bridge) in the United States, unless Connecticut's Pearl Harbor Memorial Bridge is completed first. The city is building this pedestrian overpass to link Lair Hill with the neighborhood condominium development, South Waterfront. To serve the expected five-story height and compensate for the elevation difference at the bridge's ends, an elevator and bicycle-friendly stairway are planned at South Waterfront east plaza. Existing demand estimates indicate usage could be 3,000 to 4,000 crossings per day by 2035.

## RIVER VIEW CEMETERY

In 1882, a group of prominent downtown Portland merchants founded River View Cemetery. Soon, it became the preferred eternal resting place for many of the city's elite. On the cottonwood-, alder-, and dogwood-shaded grounds of River View—which overlooks the Willamette and distant mountain summits—tombstones mark the graves of prominent Portland residents. Henry Weinhard has a stone altar; Captain John Heard Couch, a headstone festooned with chains connected to an anchor biting into the grass; and Simon Benson, a marble headstone etched with a four-bowl Benson Bubbler. The most visited grave is the pillow-shape headstone of Virgil W. Earp, the brother of Wyatt Earp who died of pneumonia and was laid to rest at River View in 1905 by his daughter, Portland resident Janie Law. Although architect Pietro Belluschi, who died on Valentine's Day 1994, chose not to be buried here, he did leave a monument—the cemetery's chapel, which he designed in the 1940s.

The red brick gatehouse that stands near the main entrance of River View Cemetery was built in 1916 and is used as an office.

The Portland Lumber Company is pictured here circa 1910. The smoke-belching business supplied the growing city of Portland—and the world, as evidenced by the ship moored to the mill's docks—with a steady stream of lumber. Also, sawdust from the mill, which was built in the 1880s, fired the boilers of a steam plant that provided heat and electricity for downtown office buildings.

# SOUTH WATERFRONT

The Portland Lumber Company and Lincoln Power Plant was located on 73 acres of the Willamette Riverfront at the southern tip of present-day Tom McCall Waterfront Park, not far from the place where founder Asa Lovejoy beached his canoe in 1843. In 1888, it fired up its boilers. For nearly a century, the smoke-belching factory churned out lumber that built the city, as well as steam and electricity that heated and powered downtown businesses. Over a 22-year period that began in 1979—three years after the demolition of the Harbor Drive Freeway—the city reinvented the mill site as RiverPlace, a riverfront rental community with a hotel, marina, and a promenade populated with dozens of cafes and boutiques. A streetcar line began servicing the area in 2005.

In 2003, buoyed by the success of RiverPlace and the Pearl District and fueled by the city's housing boom, developers turned their attention to another brownfield just upstream, a 130-acre abandoned shipyard littered with anchor chains and the bones of rusting old barges—the last major undeveloped plot of land in the central city. Known as South Waterfront, the industrial wasteland became one of the largest urban renewal projects in the nation. Within a decade, the land sprouted four steel and glass condominium towers modeled after similar developments in Vancouver, British Columbia, a streetcar line, a 16-story medical research center for Oregon Health & Science University (the city's largest employer), and an aerial tramway to link the center with its main campus atop Marquam Hill.

### RiverPlace

In 2001, the city finished redeveloping the 73-acre brownfield where the lumber mill and steam plant once stood as RiverPlace, a riverfront neighborhood with 480 apartments and condominiums, a 74-room hotel, an esplanade with boutiques and restaurants, and an 83-slip marina. The Strand Condominiums *(shown at right),* opened in 2008.

## South Waterfront

In 2007, the first homeowners began moving to a high-profile new address in South Waterfront (a.k.a. The River Blocks): The John Ross (pictured at left), a 31-story elliptically shaped condominium tower designed by Robert Thompson, the Portland architect who drafted Phil Knight's Nike corporate campus in nearby Beaverton. Buying into Southwest Portland's freshly minted neighborhood comes at a price, however. Even during the depths of the recession in the spring of 2009, a three-bedroom, 3,500-square-foot penthouse on the 30th floor of The John Ross listed for a dollar shy of $2 million. As the condominium's web site puts it: "Manhattan is SOHO, Tribeca and the East Village. San Francisco is the Haight, Mission District, SOMA and Nob Hill. Portland is the Pearl, Hawthorne and NW 23rd...and now, The River Blocks."

The Portland Streetcar makes a loop around the South Waterfront neighborhood before heading back to Portland's Nob Hill neighborhood.

## Portland Aerial Tram

The Portland Aerial Tram (foreground) approaches the upper terminal at Oregon Health & Science University's Kohler Pavilion at the summit of Marquam Hill. The tram, traveling at 22 m.p.h., whisks doctors, nurses, hospital patients, and joyriders from the university's South Waterfront campus to Kohler Pavilion, traversing 3,300 linear feet (gaining 500 feet in altitude) over the Lair Hill neighborhood in just three minutes. The gleaming pedestrian bridge (background) spans a 660-foot-long chasm between the university and the Portland Veterans Affairs Medical Center (at left).

## WILLIAM JOHNSON CABIN

IN SOUTH WATERFRONT, ELIZABETH CARUTHERS PARK is a $2.8 million, two-square-block of green space named for a pioneer who purchased the property in 1850 from the area's earliest resident. At its edge rests a relocated historical marker: a plaque affixed to a boulder that says, simply, "Site of Portland's first cabin built in 1842 by William Johnson, a sailor on Old Ironsides in the War of 1812."

Johnson, a Navy veteran who had served aboard the USS *Constitution*, took a Native American wife and, in 1842, built a log cabin in the shadows of the present-day condos, as historian Harvey Scott put it, "smuggling his domicile in an opening in the timber where a stream made the spot inimical to the fir trees."

Johnson may have been the city's first settler, but he never amounted to much. After being arrested for using molasses to brew moonshine called "blue ruin," Johnson disappeared and was promptly forgotten. So was his marker, which for decades sat on an ivy-infested embankment on an Interstate on-ramp a few blocks from the waterfront. Today, the memorial to the city's first permanent settler has a new home and the distinction of being the centerpiece of the city's newest park.

This marker honoring the first Portland log cabin awaits installation at South Waterfront's Elizabeth Caruthers Park.

# PORTLAND'S BROOKLYN

James B. Stephens, one of the most endearing figures in Portland's early history, arrived in Oregon belatedly, having just missed the 1843 wagon train from Missouri after selling his Indiana farm. Stephens, a cooper of modest ambition and limited business sense and dogged by a persistent streak of bad luck, set up a shop in The Clearing the year Portland received its name. Before Overton sold half of his claim to Pettygrove, he had first offered it to Stephens for the price of 300 salmon barrels, with two years to deliver.

But Stephens, who was known as Uncle Jimmy, had his eye on the landing on the opposite riverbank, present-day Southeast Portland, where the road to Oregon City threaded from the eastern shore of the Willamette into, as one contemporary historian described, "the darkest and thickest of forests … the mudholes . . . as had been opened scarcely dried the summer long."

No matter.

"What do you want with that land, Mr. Stephens? You have the best trade in Oregon now," asked settler John Minto, a woodsman, one of the many who sought refuge from the rain and cold in Stephens's workshop. "Yes," Stephens replied, "But from my boyhood, I have always wanted to own an orchard."

So Stephens said no thanks to Overton and invested in a square mile of land on the Willamette's inaccessible eastern shore, settled into a decrepit cabin, and there put down roots and planted an orchard.

## STEPHENS STAYS THE COURSE

A short walk from his riverfront cabin, Stephens established a ferry service, first with a rowboat, then with an elaborate horse-powered paddlewheel skiff, charging 25 cents per horse and rider, each

*Left:* In this photograph, taken in the late 1800s, the two-story whitewashed home of East Portland founder James B. Stephens, visible in the middle of the frame on the opposite bank of the river, was the most impressive building in the fledgling city of East Portland.

Image cropped

One of the reasons East Portland remained relatively undeveloped while Portland thrived was the fact that much of its waterfront was mired in swampland and split by vast gulches, which required the construction of an expensive—and architecturally challenging—network of elevated roadways, such as the trestle that spanned Hawthorne Springs, shown here in 1874.

way. During the Yakima War, he ferried regiments of the U.S. Army's cavalry back and forth in exchange for worthless paper currency. He went to California during the gold rush in 1848 and built a bridge over the American River that promptly washed away. The next year, he lost $16,000 ($434,000 today) when he sent a load of lumber to a California investor who was mired in debt, and the shipment was confiscated and distributed among creditors. Undaunted, Stephens platted out his town in 1851 and turned to real estate, placing an advertisement in East Portland's bimonthly newspaper, the *Democratic Era*, offering "land and lumber without any money down, and on three year's credit." Despite his mounting losses, in 1864, Stephens still managed to build a handsome two-story house on the riverfront that, for decades, would remain the most impressive building on the east bank. By 1870, 25 years after he crossed the river, he finally incorporated his town and gave it a name: East Portland. Aside from Stephens's home—along with three hotels, a tannery, four stores, and a tavern—the most prominent East Portland institution was Doc Hawthorne's Lunatic Asylum. But East Portland (population 830) had one thing Portland (population 8,293), which was then hemmed by insurmountable hills, desperately desired: access to a railroad. On September 10, 1883, Engine No. 154, the first transcontinental Northern Pacific Railroad locomotive

steamed into East Portland. Portland was joined to the East Coast of the United States, and by 1890, the city's population would grow five-fold.

## COME TO EAST PORTLAND!

For East Portland, the true milestone happened two years before Stephens's death, with the advance that would put his one shrewd investment—the ferry—out of business: the Morrison Bridge, the first bridge over the Willamette, which opened in 1887. Almost overnight, East Portland's population ballooned to 10,000.

The first Northern Pacific transcontinental locomotive draws onlookers at a stop en route to East Portland from St. Paul, Minnesota, in 1883.

The day before the bridge opened, *The Oregonian* said that East Portland "is the breathing spot of a commercial city." The article also noted that rooms rented for a third of what they did in downtown Portland, and lots could be had for a tenth of what they were selling for in the city. Not surprisingly, a full page of real estate advertisements followed.

## COMBINING FORCES

In 1891, two years after Stephens died, the City of Portland merged with East Portland and Albina, another east-bank city to the north. In so doing, Portland grew from its initial 16 acres, platted in 1845, to more than 16,000 acres on both banks of the river. With a population of 63,000, Portland was, for a brief time, the second largest city on the West Coast, after San Francisco. Sellwood, a riverfront village on East Portland's southern boundary, joined the city in 1893, followed 12 years later by Mount Tabor, a community that had evolved around the flanks of a cinder cone on East Portland's easternmost fringes.

Today, the majority of the city's population of 537,000 lives on the east side of the river. And Stephens's house, unlike those of the founders of downtown Portland, survives. It's located on a leafy street just off Southeast Stephens, a few blocks from Asylum Avenue (now renamed Hawthorne Boulevard) and anchors one of the trendiest neighborhoods in the city. Stephens's house still stands as the oldest in Portland's city limits, a testament to the founder *The Oregonian* eulogized as "a man made of stern material, he was very useful in the early days when robust courage was needed to make a home in the wilderness." And Stephens's woodsman friend remembered him as someone "who liked company and conversation and had shavings to burn."

*Above:* By 1895, just eight years after the construction of the Morrison Bridge (foreground) and four years after East Portland's merger with the City of Portland, practically every square foot of available land along the Willamette's east bank had been developed. The pervasiveness of flooding is evidenced by the number of buildings squatting on stilts and elevated roadways snaking along the waterfront.

The panorama of the Hawthorne District (and downtown Portland in the distance), unfolds beyond a municipal reservoir, as seen from the summit of Mount Tabor. Aside from Bend's Powell Butte, Southeast Portland's Mount Tabor (a cinder cone named for a promontory in Palestine) is the only volcano that lies within the limits of a major Oregon city.

# SOUTHEAST WATERFRONT

East Portland slumbered while downtown Portland exploded into being on the west bank of the Willamette during the mid- to late-19th century. It was due largely to the fact that much of the east side's waterfront was a forbidding swampland. Historian Harvey Scott described the scene in 1890 this way: "At the site of East Portland, three profound chasms or gulches unite to form an alluvial bottom with easy ingress from the river, but a bad water front... The strip of alluvium in front of East Portland, at the mouth of the gulches, is but a few hundred paces across, and thence the surface rises easily, nowhere attaining an elevation of more than one hundred feet, and develops into a plain with many variations leading out three miles further to Mt. Tabor. This is a solitary hill seven hundred feet in height with a commanding front and long approaches. Its slopes are most inviting for residence property, the soil is congenial to gardens and orchard trees, and its rocks of basalt give birth to a multitude of delicious springs."

As Portland grew, East Portland's waterfront remained a swampy morass, crisscrossed with wooden roadways erected on stilts. After the completion of the Morrison Bridge in 1887 and the Madison Bridge (now the Hawthorne) four years later, East Portland merged with downtown, and streetcars opened the "delicious springs and congenial soils" of Mount Tabor's slopes to development. But even after the chasms were filled and the streams were channeled underground, the east side's waterfront was still an inhospitable place, populated with unsightly warehouses, factories, docks, and by the 1960s, an elevated freeway. The waterfront renaissance began in 1992, when Oregon Museum of Science and Industry (OMSI) relocated from Washington Park into Station L, a shuttered Portland General Electric power plant in the shadows of the Marquam Bridge. It ended nine years later with the unveiling of the Vera Katz Eastbank Esplanade, an ingenious waterfront promenade floating on pontoons and cantilevered on stilts, evoking the roadways that first bridged the chasms more than a century ago.

Portland General Electric Company built a steam-powered electricity-generation plant on the east bank of the Willamette in 1910. It was shuttered in the 1970s. In 1986, PGE donated the derelict power plant, along with 18.5 acres of riverfront property, to the Oregon Museum of Science and Industry.

The Oregon Museum of Science and Industry retained historic details like the Station L's 120-foot-tall red smoke stack above the main entrance hall.

In 1992, local architecture firm Zimmer Gunsul Frasca (which two years earlier had completed the Oregon Convention Center 1.7 miles downriver in the Lloyd District) reincarnated the Station L power plant as the Oregon Museum of Science and Industry, preserving architectural details but adding a glass pyramid atrium to connect the old powerhouse (the building on the left with the red smokestack) with a domed Omnimax Theater and a modern exhibition wing (the building on the right). It is 60,000 square feet in all. The USS *Blueback,* a restored Cold War–era Navy submarine, can be seen moored at the end of the pier, just upstream from the riverboat. "The building is an allegory to the history of science and industry in the state of Oregon," designer Bob Frasca told *The Oregonian* in October 1992. "It was part of the past, and it was our intention to show the future."

Intake pipes have been preserved in the aptly named Turbine Hall at the Oregon Museum of Science and Industry. They once sucked water from the Willamette River to feed the steam-driven generators of Portland General Electric's decommissioned Station L powerplant.

## Floating Walkway

In October 1998, the City of Portland broke ground on the Eastbank Esplanade, a 1.5-mile-long waterfront promenade that would serve as the East Side's equivalent of Tom McCall Waterfront Park. The two together create a continuous three-mile loop through both parks from the Hawthorne to Steel bridges. The Esplanade, completed in 2001, used a number of innovative engineering solutions to stitch together the previously inaccessible waterfront. A catwalk was cantilevered over the river atop a mound of concrete left over from the last reconstruction of the Morrison Bridge, and a floating walkway *(left)*—the longest such structure in the United States—was built to traverse a quarter-mile stretch of shoreline that had been sacrificed as a right of way for the Interstate 5 freeway. "On the advent of Portland's 150th birthday, I am thrilled we're giving ourselves the gift of reconnecting the Willamette River, and reuniting the city's east and west sides," said Mayor Vera Katz at the dedication ceremony on May 25, 2001. "I am excited for the Central Eastside, which has waited a long time to get its own waterfront park. The Esplanade will serve as a catalyst for the neighborhood's rebirth."

This photograph shows Southeast Portland's gritty industrial waterfront between the Burnside Bridge (visible at far left) and the Morrison Bridge near the turn of the century. In 1914, a municipal dock, the port of Portland's Terminal 2, was built just upriver from the Nickum & Kelly sand and gravel business pictured here. Today, remnants of the terminal's concrete pier have been transformed into artwork along the Eastbank Esplanade that serves as a reminder of the site's maritime past.

Portland Mayor Vera Katz doggedly shepherded the design and construction of the Vera Katz Eastbank Esplanade during her two terms as mayor from 1993 to 2005. This life-size bronze statue of Katz sits near the southern entrance to the 1.5-mile-long linear riverfront park. Parkgoers often show their appreciation by dressing the bas-relief of Portland's much-loved 49th mayor—by local sculptor Bill Bane—in castoff hats, scarves, sweaters, and coats during the bone-chilling rainy season.

The Eastbank Esplanade is shown here looking south from the Morrison Bridge. The $30.5 million development is a pedestrian-friendly modern update of the elaborate network of viaducts that once bridged the east side's inaccessible waterfront in the late 19th century. During peak summer months, it attracts between 1,500 to 2,000 bicyclists a day.

# LADD'S ADDITION

When the Madison Street Bridge opened in 1891, a developer named William Sargent Ladd, who twice served as Portland's mayor in the 1850s, purchased a 126-acre tract from East Portland founder James B. Stephens. Ladd made his enduring stamp on the city with a unique subdivision known as Ladd's Addition. Eschewing Portland's rigid streetscape grid, Ladd borrowed a page from Pierre L'Enfant after visiting the District of Columbia and carved his subdivision—bounded on the north and south by present-day Hawthorne and Division streets and east and west by 20th and 12th avenues—into a wagon wheel pattern, with streets branching off in all directions from a traffic circle at the tract's very center. Ladd never lived to see his vision realized; it was completed

William Sargent Ladd

in the 1920s, and he died in 1893. But Ladd's Addition remains one of Southeast Portland's most distinctive neighborhoods, especially when viewed from above. Historian Eugene Snyder once described Ladd's Addition as "an orderly geometric form—a rectangle crossed by two diagonals, which divide the plat into four isosceles triangles. Those are further divided into smaller triangles, quadrilaterals, parallelograms, and trapezoids. Seen from the air, the subdivision looks like a British flag laid out on the checkerboard street grid of Portland's East Side." To the dozens of wayward motorists who lose themselves every day in the confounding geometry of Ladd's Addition, it seems more like the Bermuda Triangle.

In 1946, the city's most celebrated architect, Pietro Belluschi, began sketching designs for a modernist sanctuary for the blue-collar Italian American congregation of St. Philip Neri in Ladd's Addition. Modeled after early Christian brick basilicas from Roman times, Belluschi's church, except for a single rose window, was devoid of ornamentation. He once again broke the mold with the blank façade capped with a tiny of cross and a campanile that looks more like the obelisk from *2001: A Space Odyssey* than a traditional bell tower. The church was dedicated in 1952.

## Ladd's Addition

An aerial photograph taken on November 9, 1950, illustrates how radically William Sargent Ladd's 1891 spoke-and-wheel, X-shaped plat for Ladd's Addition departs from the east side's rigid north-south-east-west uniform streetscape grid. "Ladd's Addition can be something of a shock for the uninitiated," writes Bart King in *An Architectural Guidebook to Portland.* "The usual residential block pattern of a neighborhood layout has been transmogrified into a radial street network.... Confusion turns into pleasure as the pedestrian realizes that the neighborhood turns in upon itself, in order to focus on a natural 'hub.' It forms a clearly distinct neighborhood that is utterly unique, even insular."

# HAWTHORNE

Southeast Portland's most vibrant commercial strip takes its name from James C. Hawthorne, a psychiatrist and two-term senator from California. In 1862, he founded the state's first mental institution after being awarded a lucrative government contract to house "all indigent insane and idiotic persons sent to them by the county court." It was called the Oregon Hospital for the Insane, but locals called it Hawthorne's Lunatic Asylum.

A handsome two-story estate on a 24-acre wooded tract (with a spring-fed creek donated by East Portland founder James B. Stephens), it was bordered by present-day Hawthorne and Taylor on the north and south, between 9th and 12th avenues. The hospital opened with 12 patients and quickly expanded, adding another floor and two wings, with 11 wards, rooms for 100 patients, a bakery, a vegetable garden, ten cows, and 40 hogs "fattening for the winter." An inspector in 1870 declared Hawthorne's sanctuary to be "admirably fitted to insure the health, comfort and enjoyment of its inmates ... while it is sufficiently removed from the busy haunts of trade to give that quietness necessary to the disturbed and perverted minds that seek its shelter."

By 1877, Hawthorne was treating 230 patients and had achieved national renown, even attracting a visit from New York City's legendary mental health crusader, Dorothea Dix. Hawthorne died at age 61 in 1881, and was buried in nearby Lone Fir Pioneer Cemetery, where many of his patients also were laid to rest. Two years later, the state closed the facility and transferred the hospital's patients to a much larger state asylum in Salem. In 1888, the city of East Portland changed the name of the boulevard fronting the hospital from Asylum Road to Hawthorne Boulevard. After the abandoned hospital building burned down, the grounds became a public park—Hawthorne Park—which, after being passed over as a site for the Lewis and Clark Centennial Exposition, was sold off to developers and carved up as lots for new homes.

Hawthorne Boulevard has evolved into one of the trendiest—and most bohemian—commercial strips in the city. Stretching from the flanks of Mount Tabor (visible in the background) to the east bank of the Willamette, restaurants, tattoo parlors, coffee houses, brewpubs, boutiques, and more recently, condominiums have sprouted along the boulevard, which branches out into a leafy residential enclave populated with lovingly restored craftsman bungalows.

In 1906, architects William Whidden and Ion Lewis replaced a former stagecoach stop at the intersection of Hawthorne Boulevard and Sommerville Road with this Georgian Revival mansion for lumber baron Philip Buehner. Since 1944, it has been the home of Western Seminary.

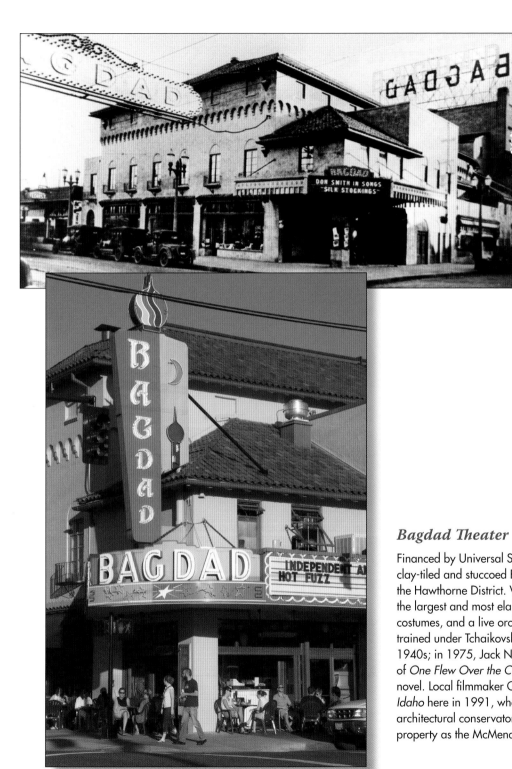

## LONE FIR PIONEER CEMETERY

IN 1846, EAST PORTLAND FOUNDER JAMES B. STEPHENS sold his family farm to Colburn Barrell, a businessman who operated a steamship line. Stephens's father, Emmor Stephens, was buried on the property, and Barrell agreed to maintain the gravesite. Eight years later, Barrell buried his business partner and other victims of the steamship *Gazelle* tragedy (its boiler had exploded while it was moored in the Willamette above Oregon City) there and set aside 30 acres as a public cemetery; he sold it to investors in 1866, and it was renamed Lone Fir. In addition to Dr. J. C. Hawthorne, the city's oldest cemetery is the final resting place of many prominent pioneers, including East Portland founder James Stephens and Portland founder Asa Lovejoy. In 1947, the county acquired a section of the cemetery that had been reserved in the 1870s "for the burial of Chinamen." After exhuming bodies and sending the remains to China for reinternment according to Chinese custom, the county built an administration office and a parking lot. When the building was demolished in 2005, workers discovered unmarked graves believed to be those of asylum patients; later, the county held public hearings to consider a proposal for a memorial on the site, honoring the Chinese who were buried there and the unknown patients of Dr. Hawthorne.

## Bagdad Theater

Financed by Universal Studios and designed by local architect Lee Thomas, the clay-tiled and stuccoed Bagdad Theater looks more like vintage Hollywood than the Hawthorne District. When it opened in 1927 *(above left)*, the Bagdad was the largest and most elaborate theater on the East Side. Ushers wore Arabian costumes, and a live orchestra performed film scores (the theater's maestro had trained under Tchaikovsky). Sammy Davis Jr. performed at the Bagdad in the 1940s; in 1975, Jack Nicholson was the guest of honor at the Oregon premiere of *One Flew Over the Cuckoo's Nest,* based on Oregonian Ken Kesey's 1962 novel. Local filmmaker Gus Van Sant debuted his breakthrough *My Own Private Idaho* here in 1991, when the theater, restored by Portland brewpub magnates/architectural conservators Mike and Brian McMenamin, rededicated the historic property as the McMenamins Bagdad Theater & Pub.

The Southern Pacific Railroad built a roundhouse in 1912 to service steam locomotives chugging into the Brooklyn Yard, the railroad's northernmost terminus, which is situated just south of Ladd's Addition. Since 1974, the "New House," a timber-framed addition to the original roundhouse (which was demolished in 1959), has served as a home to three retired steam locomotives—and a streamlined 1950s era diesel locomotive shown here—that several railroad companies donated to the city.

# BROOKLYN ROUNDHOUSE

Before the transcontinental railroad arrived in Portland, two competing companies on both sides of the river raced to build a rail link from Portland to San Francisco. The race began in April 1868, when a group of downtown investors from the Oregon Steam Navigation Company started laying track on the west bank, and the Oregon Central Railroad, backed by prominent east siders, began construction on the east bank. Bedeviled by the east side's marshy terrain, Oregon Central ran out of money within three months; the west side line declared bankruptcy a year later.

Enter California's "Stagecoach King," the deep-pocketed Ben Holladay. After selling his business and moving to Portland in 1869, he bought out the Oregon Central investors and by Christmas had completed 20 miles of the east-side line and rechristened it as the Oregon and California Railroad. The line began at a vast yard at Brookland, a 500-acre farm with springs owned by William Ladd just south of present-day Ladd's Addition, and followed the east bank of the river south through the towns of Sellwood, Oregon City, and farmland beyond. Holladay prevailed over the Oregon Steam Navigation Company and pushed all the way to Roseburg by 1873. But the stock market collapsed that year and ended his empire-building ambitions; Holladay was bought out by another railroad tycoon, Henry Villard.

Villard halted the construction of Holladay's California line and, after gaining control of Northern Pacific in 1881, began building a transcontinental route to the east. Villard steamed into East Portland on the first Northern Pacific train from Minnesota two years later, just as his empire began to crumble. After Villard's demise, Southern Pacific purchased the neglected Oregon and California line and quickly completed the link to the California border. The first steam locomotive from San Francisco arrived in East Portland in December 1887. Brookland—which by then was known as Brooklyn—served as the northern terminus of its operations, with home sites nearby for a working class community of railroad workers. The company built locomotive shops, a turntable, and two roundhouses to service its fleet of locomotives.

In the 1950s, when the nation's railroads scrapped cantankerous steam locomotives in favor of more efficient diesel power, the city acquired three of the steam engines, which have been stored in the Brooklyn Roundhouse (now owned by Union Pacific) since the 1970s. Over the years, a volunteer group of retired engineers and steam train enthusiasts—calling itself the Oregon Rail Heritage Foundation—has restored two of the old steam beasts to working order. Several times a year they fire up the boilers and send the trains trundling out of the roundhouse and along the waterfront; the winsome sound of their steam whistles resurrects the ghosts and lost ambitions of Holladay and Villard.

Two mammoth Southern Pacific locomotives steam out of the Brooklyn Yard in the 1940s. The roundhouse, which is the center building visible in the background, was built during World War II and is the last roundhouse in the city. Since 1974, it has served as headquarters of the Oregon Rail Heritage Foundation, a group of volunteers dedicated to maintaining and restoring three vintage steam locomotives owned by the City of Portland.

The pride and joy of Portland's locomotive collection is the 4449, shown here chugging out of Spokane, Washington, en route to Sandpoint, Idaho. The locomotive, which was built in 1941 and weighs 237 tons, pulled Southern Pacific passenger trains between Los Angeles and Portland until it was retired from service in 1958. After languishing outside Oaks Amusement Park, the locomotive was donated to the city and moved to the Brooklyn Roundhouse in 1974, where it was restored in time to pull the 1976 Bicentennial Freedom Train across the United States. It's the last operational "streamliner" steam locomotive from the Art Deco era in the world.

In 1892, President Warren G. Harding established the Bull Run Reserve, restricting development in Mount Hood's pristine Bull Run watershed, the source of Portland's drinking water. Dam 1 on the 10-billion-gallon Bull Run Reservoir 1 (also known as Lake Ben Morrow) is shown here after its completion in 1929. It was designed by D. C. Henny, who went on to serve as consulting engineer for the Hoover Dam.

One of Mount Tabor's three century-old reservoirs is still used to store the city's unfiltered drinking water, piped underground from pristine Bull Run in the heart of the Mount Hood National Forest. Forced to comply with federal public health rules that prohibit the storage of drinking water in open pools—a concern heightened when two skinny-dippers were caught in the reservoir—the city has proposed capping Mount Tabor's signature water features, a move that's vehemently opposed by park users and neighborhood residents.

# MOUNT TABOR

In 1848, an itinerant Methodist preacher named Clinton Kelly claimed 640 acres on the flanks of a cinder cone a mile east of the Willamette River. Six years later, when Methodist families formed a church, the minister's son, who had been reading *Napoleon and His Marshals,* supplied the church name, a name for the cinder cone, and a name for the burgeoning town that sprung up around it: Mount Tabor, after the hillside in Palestine where Napoleon's Christian forces had battled the armies of Islam. The Kellys and other settlers eventually divvied up their hillside holdings and sold off lots to waves of prospective homeowners that flooded the east side in the late 1880s and 1890s. They were no doubt inspired by *The Oregonian*'s lengthy article devoted to East Portland real estate published five days before the Morrison Street Bridge's dedication on April 12, 1887: "Not within a radius of miles can such beautiful and sightly spots be found…making it a lovely and picturesque location for homes."

Homes sprouted up and down the mountain's flanks, encroaching on Mount Tabor's then privately owned and undeveloped 240-acre summit promontory. In 1903, landscape designer John C. Olmsted urged Portland's Park Board to acquire the property as a public greenspace, Mount Tabor Park, which happened in 1912, seven years after the city annexed the area.

The gatehouse of Mount Tabor Reservoir Number 1 is shown here in 1912, the year the city acquired the dormant volcano as a public park. To secure a permanent supply of drinking water, the City of Portland employed an army of unemployed laborers to build Conduit 1, a pipeline 24 miles long that runs from the Bull Run Reservoir (a pristine glacier-fed lake on the flanks of Mount Hood) to Reservoir 1. It was completed in 1894. Water from Bull Run began flowing into the 12-million-gallon Mount Tabor reservoir on January 2, 1895.

Homes crowd the perimeter of Mount Tabor Park, which was protected from development in 1912. It was partly due to John C. Olmsted, who urged city leaders in 1903 to acquire the tract, noting, "It is the only important landscape feature for miles around. It is already a good deal resorted to by people for their Sunday and holiday outings…There can be little doubt that public sentiment will cordially support the city government in acquiring considerable land on this prominent and beautiful hill."

## HARVEY W. SCOTT

HARVEY W. SCOTT WAS A 27-YEAR-OLD PORTLAND *arriviste* from Illinois by way of Puget Sound. He was working as a librarian when, in 1865, he caught the eye of *Oregonian* publisher Henry Pittock by penning "The Great Atrocity," a eulogy for Abraham Lincoln; Pittock published it as an editorial two days after the president was assassinated. Pittock was so impressed, he installed Scott as the newspaper's editor a year later. For more than 40 years, Scott was the most powerful (and typically acerbic) journalistic voice in Oregon and the Pacific Northwest. He was an unabashed conservative who used his prominence to promote segregation ("If we are forced to have Chinese residents, let them occupy some quarter designated apart from the best and most prominent places in the city.") and, to the dismay of his sister, activist Abigail Scott Duniway, opposed suffrage for women. Gutzon Borglum created a statue of Scott, taking time off from his monolithic carving of Mount Rushmore to cast Scott in bronze. The statue was gifted by Scott's widow in the 1930s and stands atop Mount Tabor today, pointing to the city across the river.

In this 1916 photo, a horse-drawn hearse and carriages of mourners queue in front of the Walter Kenworthy Funeral home on Southeast 13th Avenue in Sellwood for the funeral of Waverly Country Club's head gardener.

# SELLWOOD-MORELAND

The riverfront neighborhood now known as Sellwood-Moreland didn't have a name until 1883, when Episcopal minister John Sellwood sold a 160-acre tract of riverfront land—south of the Brooklyn rail yard and west of the Oregon and California Railroad tracks—to a real estate company that was controlled by Henry Pittock, publisher of Portland's daily newspaper, *The Oregonian*. Pittock traded on the legend of Sellwood, who had achieved hero status by being gravely wounded during the Watermelon War (an 1856 Panama City uprising against American

pioneers transiting the Panamanian isthmus), naming both his real estate venture and the town site after the revered reverend. In an 1887 article extolling the virtues of East Side real estate, *The Oregonian* reminded readers of the townsite's noble namesake: "Mr. Sellwood escaped with his life by almost a miracle, but was shot, most fearfully and brutally beaten and mutilated by the fiendish natives, who left him on the ground supposing he was dead. In consideration of these outrages, the government donated the land." The paper also promoted the Sellwood

enclave to its readers as "one of the most pleasantly situated suburban towns on either side of the Willamette. Though younger than any of her sister towns across the river, Sellwood enjoys a very prosperous present and looks forward to a future as bright and encouraging as any in the whole country."

Nevertheless, due to its isolation on the Willamette's east bank, several miles upriver from downtown Portland, lot sales languished until 1893, when the area was annexed by the city, and the construction of a new power station

on the Willamette Falls in Oregon City spawned an interurban railroad that brought electric trolley service to Sellwood and cities beyond. At the turn of the century, Sellwood flourished as a working class streetcar suburb; meanwhile, on the east side of the tracks, in 1910, the Ladd Estate Company began marketing William Ladd's Crystal Springs Farm acreage as Eastmoreland, an exclusive subdivision that the company's real estate maps promised would be "forever endowed with wealth and wisdom."

## *Waverly Country Club*

Waverly Country Club was founded in 1896 on makeshift links near present-day Cleveland High School. It moved two years later to its present location on the banks of the Willamette just upstream from the Sellwood Ferry landing (at the foot of present-day Sellwood bridge). The clubhouse at Waverly Country Club was built in 1913. Waverly, pictured circa 1920 above and today at right, was the first golf club in Oregon and is one of the oldest country clubs in the United States.

## *Sellwood Bridge*

When the Sellwood Bridge (pictured today) opened in 1925, it put the *John F. Caples* steam ferry out of business. Although it's the busiest two-lane bridge in the state today, it's also one of the most decrepit. In 2004, engineers discovered that the bridge (which incorporated girders recycled from the 1894 Burnside Bridge) was so riddled with cracks and structural defects that they downgraded its weight limit, barring buses, trucks, and even fire engines from using the span. Although a task force voted to replace the bridge in early 2009, government officials have struggled to raise the $280 to $360 million needed to rebuild it.

## OAKS PIONEER CHURCH

**BUILT IN 1851 ON LAND DONATED** by pioneer Lot Whitcomb in the present-day town of Milwaukie, St. John's Episcopal Church narrowly escaped demolition in 1961, when preservationists raised $4,300 and floated the building two miles downriver to the former Sellwood Ferry slip at the end of Southeast Spokane Street. From there, the church was towed two blocks uphill and deposited at the edge of Sellwood Park, where it was reassembled, renovated, and reincarnated as the Oaks Pioneer Church, now the most popular marriage venue in the city, minting around 300 new couples every year.

In 1936, the city purchased a 45-acre parcel of undeveloped land bordering Eastmoreland Golf Course; using funds and laborers from the Works Progress Administration, Westmoreland Park was built. The 143,000 square foot concrete pool below the athletic fields (which are still being graded), lower left, is the park's yet-to-be-filled casting pond.

Westmoreland Park's refurbished casting pond is one of the few artificial casting ponds in the United States. In 2001, a ruptured wooden pipe that fed the pond from nearby Crystal Springs Creek was deemed too expensive to repair. The empty pond languished while the city searched for an alternate water source. Anglers (and mallards) returned in October 2006, when excess spring water diverted from city-owned Eastmoreland Golf Course refilled the pond.

In 1951, visitors inspect the blooms of Crystal Springs Rhododendron Garden. In 1950, the Portland Chapter of the American Rhododendron Society of America had transformed Shakespeare Island into an international rhododendron test garden.

A footbridge in Westmoreland Park spans Crystal Springs Creek, which burbles from the ground in nearby Reed College and winds its way through the neighborhood.

Bikers, joggers, and strollers converge on the Springwater Corridor Trail, a 21-mile-long, mostly paved pedestrian and bicycle path that begins near the Eastbank Esplanade and follows tracks through wetlands to Oaks Amusement Park. From there, the route follows the right of way of an abandoned interurban line to Gresham, passing through two nature preserves and ultimately shunting bicyclists onto the road to Mount Hood. It is an integral part of the 40 Mile Loop, a network of trails circumnavigating the city.

From 1905 to 1920 (when it was destroyed by a fire), Shoot the Chutes was one of the most popular attractions at Oaks Amusement Park. Thrill seekers rode an escalator to the top of the platform, where they boarded flat-bottomed boats that careened down the "chute" and into a shallow pond.

# OAKS AMUSEMENT PARK

Hoping to capitalize on the multitudes expected to visit Portland's 1905 exposition and lure streetcar riders during the evening and weekend off-hours at the same time, an east side interurban line known as the Oregon Water Power & Railway Company began building an amusement park on 44 oak-shrouded acres along Sellwood's riverfront in 1904. Modeled after New York City's Coney Island, Oaks Amusement Park opened on May 30, 1905, two days before the Lewis and Clark Centennial Exposition, and surpassed the railway's most optimistic projections. Over the next four months, more than 300,000 revelers paid five cents each to board Oregon Water Power & Railway's open-air excursion cars and forked over another ten cents to partake of the Oaks midway, tavern, dancing pavilion, and thrill rides such as Shoot the Chutes, a rickety seven-story wooden platform that sent riders down a ramp into a pond. On a Monday night in August that year, a crowd of 10,000 also anted up an extra 50 cents ($12 today) to watch Henry J. Pain, a local fireworks impresario, recreate the destruction of Pompeii on a three-acre stage complete with a scale model of the doomed ancient city populated by toga-clad actors and acrobats and a gunpowder-fueled volcano—a spectacle Pain promoted as "the greatest and grandest, most elaborate, gigantic, extravagant, interesting, thrilling and gorgeous, historical, Biblical, dramatic, musical, scenic, spectacular and pyrotechnical open-air exhibition the world has ever witnessed."

Although the streetcar stopped running in 1958 (bikers, rollerbladers, and joggers now know the former trolley line as the Springwater Trail), the Oaks, one of the oldest continuously operated amusement parks in America, still attracts more than 450,000 visitors every year.

Revelers stroll the midway at Oaks Amusement Park, circa 1908. The Oregon Water Power & Railway Company opened the park along its Oregon City trolley line on Sellwood's riverfront in 1905. The fountain lamp visible on the right was one of the many artifacts—including a band shell—that the park purchased from the fairgrounds, which were dismantled in 1906.

Each year, nearly half a million thrill-seekers come to Oaks Amusement Park, ranking Portland's century-old version of Coney Island just behind southern Oregon's Crater Lake National Park as one of the state's most popular tourist attractions.

# REED COLLEGE

Architect A. E. Doyle based his 1920 master plan for Reed College on Oxford University's Saint John's College, giving the campus an outwardly Ivy League feel by adopting a conventional Tudor style for the original cluster of academic buildings. However, Reed's Classics-oriented, non-grade-based liberal arts curriculum has earned the school a reputation as a maverick institution that one former *New York Times* education editor deemed "the most intellectual college in the country." Critics, however, disdain it as pretentious: In 2008, *Radar* magazine voted Reed, after Swarthmore College, the nation's "most insufferable" institution of higher learning.

Locals mistakenly believe the school was named after Portland's most notorious communist activist, John Reed—the journalist who penned *Ten Days That Shook the World* in 1919 and is entombed with Communist heroes outside the Kremlin. It was actually named after philanthropist Simeon Gannett Reed, a business partner of east side developer William Ladd. His widow bequeathed 40 acres of Ladd's Crystal Springs Farm holdings to the "Reed Institute" in 1904. Adding to the college's nonconformist status, the dominant physical feature of the Reed campus isn't a leafy quadrangle but a twisting canyon: a wildlife preserve where Crystal Springs burbles from the ground to fill one of the only naturally occurring lakes left within the city limits. The space is used as an outdoor classroom to teach biology.

A. E. Doyle's Tudor-style dormitory, one of the first buildings to rise out of the pastures of a stock farm that became Reed College. The Old Dorm (as it's now known), conspicuous on yet-to-be-developed pastureland, is pictured here in 1915, three years after the first undergrads moved in.

A. E. Doyle, the architect of Portland's Central Library, used Oxford's St. John's College as the inspiration for Reed College's earliest academic buildings, but his design of the 1912 Old Dorm residence hall, with its slate roof and massive brick chimneys, evokes a stately English manor home.

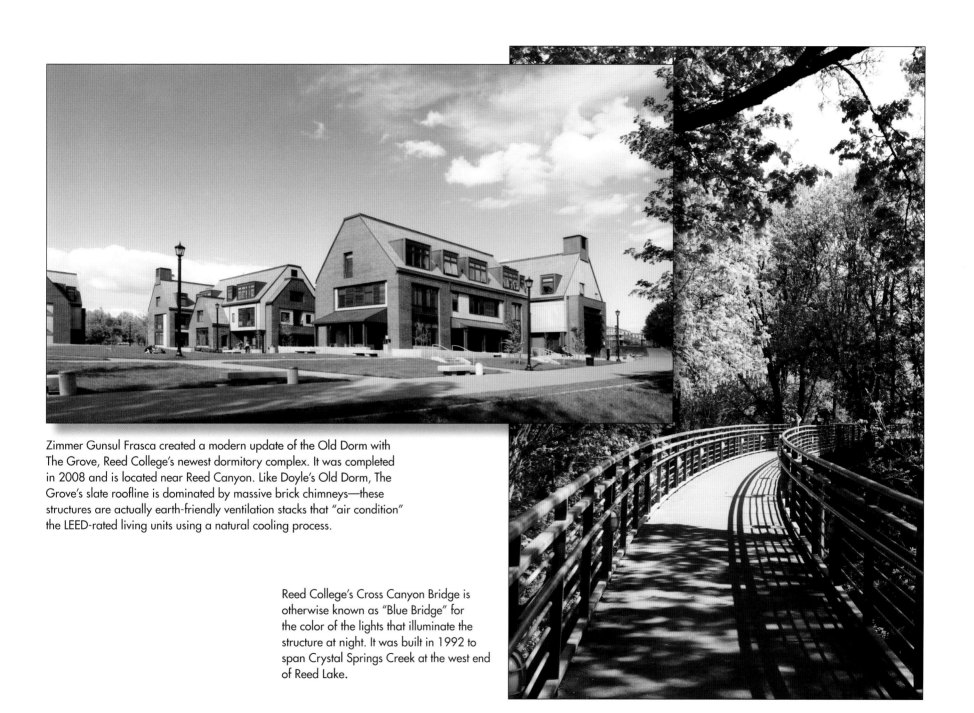

Zimmer Gunsul Frasca created a modern update of the Old Dorm with The Grove, Reed College's newest dormitory complex. It was completed in 2008 and is located near Reed Canyon. Like Doyle's Old Dorm, The Grove's slate roofline is dominated by massive brick chimneys—these structures are actually earth-friendly ventilation stacks that "air condition" the LEED-rated living units using a natural cooling process.

Reed College's Cross Canyon Bridge is otherwise known as "Blue Bridge" for the color of the lights that illuminate the structure at night. It was built in 1992 to span Crystal Springs Creek at the west end of Reed Lake.

# DIVIDING THE DINNER BUCKET

When Edwin Russell, manager of the Portland branch of the Bank of British Columbia, filed a map of his plat for the City of Albina in 1873 (as noted by historian E. Kimbark MacColl in *The Shaping of a City*), his "city" was mostly overgrown marshland at the foot of a forested bluff, with no graded streets. Seven years after its founding, Albina (Al-bEE-na), named for the wife of a prominent Portland judge, had mustered a population of only 143.

That quickly changed with the arrival of the first transcontinental railroad in 1883. The Portland-based Oregon Railway & Navigation company spent $1.5 million turning 320 acres of Albina's riverfront into a vast switchyard it leased to Union Pacific as a western terminus for transcontinental frieght trains. The arrival of the railroad, coupled with the opening of the Morrison Bridge in 1887 and the Steel Bridge two years later, transformed Albina into a boomtown. By 1888, more than 3,000 German, Russian, Italian, and Polish railroad workers had settled in what was quickly becoming Portland's primary working class enclave, thanks to the efforts of real estate magnate William Killingsworth, who became Albina's primary booster and developer.

"The great factor in city making is the laboring man—the man with the dinner bucket," Killingsworth said in an interview published in the April 6, 1888, edition of the *Morning Oregonian*. "It is he, thousands of times multiplied, that sets the dynamo in motion which furnishes the heat for the heart throbs of a city... There will be immense fortunes made in Albina property."

And none greater than the one amassed by Killingsworth himself. In 1890, he relocated from the West Side to a four-story mansion with 16 rooms in the heart of Albina that cost $25,000, a princely sum at the time, conspicuous among the slapdash bungalows of his working-class neighbors. And they

In June 1894, the Willamette River flooded Union Pacific's leased switchyard on the City of Albina's riverfront. The mammoth brick smokestack that towers above the locomotive sheds in the background, built in 1887, still stands today in the shadows of the Fremont Bridge.

*Left:* The sun sets on North Portland's industrial waterfront. The light towers in the background (beneath the arch of the Fremont Bridge) illuminate Union Pacific's riverfront switchyard at the foot of the bluffs below north Portland's Overlook neighborhood. The switchyard was established in the late 1800s as the western terminus for transcontinental freight trains.

kept coming. In 1890, Albina's population of 5,129 was a tenth of the size of Portland's. According to MacColl, a year later, Albina joined its East Portland neighbor in a merger with the City of Portland, and since it had already absorbed the village of St. Johns, it sprawled for 13.5 square miles—an area larger than East and West Portland combined. Today, Albina's historic city limits encompass 13 neighborhoods in inner North and Northeast Portland.

## A DOWNWARD SPIRAL

From 1905 to 1928, more than 20,000 homes were built for workers employed mainly by Union Pacific or the vast Union Stockyards in Kenton on the outskirts near the Columbia Slough. At the dawn of World War II, industrialist Henry Kaiser based two massive shipyards in Albina and nearby St. Johns. They became the nation's most prolific producer of Liberty Ships, freighters used to haul troops, equipment, and supplies to fronts in Europe. Between 1940 and 1944, the Kaiser shipyards and related wartime businesses recruited 160,000 workers—swelling Portland's population by a third—including 25,000 African Americans, increasing that demographic from 1 percent to 6.9 percent of the city total. Kaiser settled 30,000 of these workers (including more than 6,000 African Americans) at Vanport, a hastily built housing project—which

became the second largest city in Oregon—sited on a previously uninhabited floodplain in Albina just north of the stockyards. In 1948, after the shipyards had closed and Vanport had deteriorated into a ghetto, a flood wiped the housing project off the map, leaving 18,700 former shipyard workers homeless. Real estate agents who showed African American homebuyers property in established white neighborhoods faced expulsion from the Realty Board, which taught novice realtors in its extension course "about setting up certain districts for Negroes."

Albina railyards to build Memorial Coliseum, an arena that became the home of the Portland Trail Blazers. Four years later, another 300 families were displaced when Interstate 5 cleaved a path through the heart of Albina. In 1961, *The Oregonian* published a series of articles investigating "slum-ridden" and "blighted" Albina, neighborhoods characterized by "an unusually high proportion of crime, broken families, and disease."

Albina's downward spiral bottomed with two days of riots during the summer of 1967, when the police, backed by

Even the flood waters of the Willamette River couldn't wash away the grit of Albina's industrial waterfront, shown here in June 1894. In 1890, *Oregonian* editor Harvey Scott described the area this way: "The business part of the town aside from its great works, is of rather mean appearance, of cheap temporary structures, small-sized and of inferior architecture."

African Americans settled along down-trodden Union Avenue, a once-thriving commercial district, which had deteriorated badly after the city had shunted highway traffic onto Interstate Avenue in the 1940s. In 1956, the city of Portland evicted 150 mostly African American families from their homes near the

the FBI and the National Guard, were dispatched to the neighborhood after a mob of 200 Albina residents, protesting deteriorating conditions in the neighborhood, firebombed businesses along Union Avenue, and another crowd in Irving Park began pelting cars with rocks and bottles.

## AWAKENING ALBINA

In the aftermath, the city initiated an urban renewal program, which sputtered along until the next turn of the century, when young creative professionals from across the country started moving to Portland. Drawn by its thriving downtown, they began looking for inexpensive housing that offered a quick commute to jobs in the city center. Art galleries outpriced by upscale development in the Pearl District across the river colonized Northeast Alberta Street, a commercial strip once favored by drug dealers that realtors started marketing as the Alberta Arts district, uprooting longtime African American residents to cheaper distant eastern suburbs like Gresham. In 2004, Interstate Avenue received a light rail line, breathing life into mostly white North Portland working class neighborhoods such as Kenton, where Sam Adams, the city's 51st mayor, owns a bungalow. Two years later, a former Oregon food bank warehouse on North Williams Avenue not far from Russell Street, early Albina's long-neglected Main Street, sprouted a vegan restaurant, high-end bistro, coffee roaster, and high-end children's boutique. The only anomaly is a vacant lot at the corner of Interstate and Killingsworth, which, since 2004, has defied repeated attempts by the city to jump start a 54-unit, high-rise condo named for Killingsworth himself, who once responded to a reporter questioning the wisdom of investing heavily in Albina by arguing that its "future is as sure as gravitation."

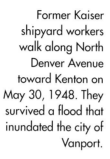

Former Kaiser shipyard workers walk along North Denver Avenue toward Kenton on May 30, 1948. They survived a flood that inundated the city of Vanport.

Freight cars are shunted onto sidings at Union Pacific's switchyard at the foot of the Fremont Bridge (background). Still known as the Albina Shops or Yards, the switchyard dates from the 1880s.

# SWAN ISLAND

During World War II, industrialist Henry Kaiser's shipyards on Swan Island, in St. Johns, and on the Columbia in Vancouver, Washington, were among the most prolific shipbuilding operations in the world; they churned out a combined total of 455 oil tankers, aircraft carrier escorts, and military freighters by war's end (many, like the *Star of Oregon*, were torpedoed by German submarines). Almost overnight, Portland had become the hub of the nation's Liberty Ship construction program, enticing tens of thousands of men and women in cities and towns across America onto Oregon-bound trains to begin new lives in North Portland, in service of their country.

More than 100,000 shipwrights at three Kaiser Yards worked in round-the-clock shifts, shattering production records. In September 1942, President Roosevelt came to Swan Island to watch his daughter smash a bottle of California bubbly over the bow of the *Joseph N. Teal*, sending the tanker down the ways at Swan Island ten days after its keel was laid.

Today, many of the grandchildren and great grandchildren of Kaiser's "soldiers of production" live on the bluffs of North Portland and work at the 580-acre Swan Island Industrial Park. The park is home to 170 mostly blue-collar businesses, including Federal Express, United Parcel Service, and Cascade General, which operates the largest ship-repair facility on the West Coast on 60 acres at the northern tip of the island, the site of the Kaiser Swan Island Shipyard's now-crumbling slipways. Cascade General typically services cruise ships, factory trawlers, oil tankers, and occasionally a rush job for the U.S. Navy. In 2008, the *Sea Fighter*, an experimental high-speed combat catamaran developed by the Department of Defense, turned heads when it was raised into Cascade General's dry dock for an overhaul. Long, gray, and squat, she may not be the most attractive ship ever berthed on Swan Island, but with a top speed of 50 knots, the Navy brags that she's the fastest little craft that ever flew upon the water.

In 1941, Henry Kaiser founded his first Portland shipyard, the Oregon Shipbuilding Company, on 87 acres in St. Johns with a contract to build freighters for the British government. Two years later, when this photograph was taken, the Kaiser St. Johns shipyard employed some 35,000 workers.

Henry Kaiser's "soldiers of production" head home at the end of the day shift. Shipwrights worked at three sprawling Kaiser Yards on Swan Island, in St. Johns, and Vancouver, Washington.

## Ship Shape

On September 25, 1942, workers at Henry Kaiser's Swan Island shipyard *(above)* lay the keel of the *Joseph N. Teal,* one of the Liberty Ships built in Portland during World War II. More than 60 years later, near the Kaiser shipyard slipways, freighters await repair at Cascade General *(below),* the largest ship repair facility on the West Coast.

## STAR OF OREGON

THREE YEARS BEFORE ASA LOVEJOY beached his canoe at the claim that would become downtown Portland, just across the river, a group of settlers hatched an audacious plan to break up the monopoly that the Hudson's Bay Company held on the region's meager supply of livestock. Loaded to the gunwales with tools and supplies, they landed on then-unnamed Swan Island near the opposite bank of the Willamette, beneath the towering bluffs of present-day North Portland. Under the direction of a trapper named Joseph Gale, the farmers began hewing timbers and laying the keel of a 53-foot Baltimore clipper. A year later, in August 1841, Gale, the son of a Philadelphia sea captain, nosed the *Star of Oregon* into the current and set sail for the mouth of the Columbia. She was the first ship built in Oregon Country and was, by Gale's account, a beauty.

It made what he had set out to do that much harder. When Gale and his crew of Willamette valley farmers arrived in San Francisco, they traded the *Star of Oregon* to a grateful French mariner whose schooner had run aground at Point Reyes. They traded 350 cows for her, which they herded more than 630 miles back to the Willamette Valley.

A century later, on May 19, 1941, another *Star of Oregon*, the state's first Liberty Ship, slid down the ways at Henry Kaiser's Oregon Shipbuilding Company just down the river in St. Johns.

# ST. JOHNS

On April 3, 1806, a detachment from Lewis and Clark's Corps of Discovery explored the northernmost tip of North Portland now known as St. Johns, a vast bluff near the confluence of the Columbia and Willamette rivers. However, the area wasn't settled until 1847, when a pioneer named James John, who had emigrated to Oregon from Missouri, filed a claim for 320 acres of the East Side riverfront, six miles downriver from Portland. John, a teetotaling recluse locals referred to as "Jimmy" or "Saint John," built a store near the foot of present-day St. Johns Bridge and filed a plat for a settlement in 1852; it was the same year John began operating a rowboat ferry service to Linnton, a rival Portland townsite across the river. John died four years later, and his plans for a thriving city failed to materialize, given the location's isolation.

In 1891, when the village was annexed by the City of Albina and then the City of Portland, only 500 people lived in the area, and the only business of note was a cooperage that shipped barrels to Hawaii. But this quickly changed after the Oregon Railway & Navigation Company extended its freight line from Albina to St. Johns in 1902, spawning an industrial boom that led to the city's secession from Portland in 1903, when an iron works, lumber mill, and the country's first plywood mill—the former barrel company—had taken root on St. Johns's waterfront.

By 1904, the industrial city's population had quadrupled to 2,000, and by 1910, its waterfront boasted a half-dozen sawmills and two shipyards, including the first dry dock on the West Coast. So prolific was the city's industrial rise that Portland annexed St. Johns back into its fold in 1915. Despite its annexation and its physical connection to Portland—the gothic-styled 1931 St. Johns Bridge, the first suspension bridge built west of the Mississippi—this working-class enclave today feels less like a small piece of the big city and more like the sleepy riverfront village Jimmy "Saint" John founded back in 1852.

In 1910, St. Johns, which had seceded from the City of Portland seven years earlier, was still more of a sleepy village than a city like Portland, six miles upriver.

St. Johns City Hall is only three years old here in 1909. After merging with the City of Portland in 1915, St. Johns no longer needed a city hall; it was converted into a fire station and later became the home of the North Precinct of the Portland Police Bureau.

## Cathedral Park

Cathedral Park is located on the St. Johns waterfront near where founder Jimmy "Saint" John first platted the town site in 1852. It draws its name from the cathedral-like footings of Portland's only suspension bridge, the St. Johns. When completed in 1931, the 1,200-foot-long St. Johns (400 feet shy of the Brooklyn Bridge) was the longest on the West Coast, a record that fell five years later to the San Francisco–Oakland Bay Bridge.

# UNIVERSITY PARK AND OVERLOOK

In 1901, Archbishop Alexander Christie, head of the Archdiocese of Portland, was transiting the Willamette by steamer when, searching for a site for a Catholic university, he spied a Gothic tower on the bluff. It was West Hall, the academic building that was home to the city's first (failed) institution of higher learning, Portland University, which had closed two years earlier as the result of a real estate deal gone bad.

The Methodist Episcopal Church had founded Portland University on the bluff in 1891. As historian Eugene Snyder notes in *Portland Names and Neighborhoods,* to finance the purchase and endow the university, the church had gone into the real estate business, acquiring 600 acres of land and platting an exclusive subdivision it marketed as University Park. Naming streets after educators and Ivy League colleges, Portland University made a handsome profit, selling off more than 3,600 lots on credit, charging just enough in interest to pay down its own debt. But like the real estate crash of 2008, the Panic of 1893 (a severe nationwide economic depression that lasted four years) forced many of the new homeowners into default, and the university, unable to make its own loan payments, went bankrupt.

Enter Archbishop Christie. After buying the property in 1901, Christie rechristened the campus Columbia University, which changed its name to the University of Portland in 1935. In 1906, entrepreneur Henry Wemme (who had made a fortune as founder of Portland's first outdoor gear business, the Willamette Tent and Awning Company), acquired the bluff land upriver from the university and developed it as Overlook. Similar to University Park, Overlook is anchored by a campus: the American headquarters of adidas. In 2002, adidas resurrected the former Bess Kaiser Hospital—the first Portland hospital built by Kaiser Permanente, an HMO that evolved from a World War II era health plan for Kaiser Shipyard workers—as the gleaming adidas Village.

The cylindrical building *(top)* serves as the gymnasium at adidas Village, the North American headquarters of adidas. Bess Kaiser Hospital *(bottom)* is still under construction here on March 4, 1959, but was dedicated in July of that year. In 2000, adidas hired Portland firm BOORA Architects to transform the shuttered hospital (which closed in 1998) into a 350,000-square-foot corporate campus for employees of its American division.

The faculty and students of Portland University, the city's first institution of higher learning, pose in front of West Hall (said to have been modeled after Harvard University's Sever Hall) in 1892, a year after the university was founded, and a year before the Panic of 1893 bankrupted the institution, which had invested heavily in real estate (the adjacent subdivision of University Park). After being sold, the school reopened as Columbia University, and became the University of Portland in 1935. West Hall is now known as Waldschmidt Hall.

## University Park Chapel

Designed by architect Pietro Belluschi in 1985, the University of Portland's Chapel of Christ the Teacher was dedicated in 1986. Belluschi, who died in 1994, regarded the chapel as one of his foremost works. "He had a real sense of the holy, an almost classic sense of the holy," University of Portland theology professor Richard Rutherford told *The Baltimore Sun*'s architecture critic two weeks after Belluschi's death. "Beauty. Order. Harmony. He could see God in those things."

The recent arrival of upscale businesses like the Cup & Saucer Café (right)—long a fixture in the trendy Hawthorne District—have signaled a renaissance for the street, as well as for Kenton, which already received a nod when its most prominent resident, city commissioner Sam Adams, was elected mayor in 2008.

# KENTON

In 1906, St. Louis–based meatpacking conglomerate Swift & Company purchased 3,400 acres along the Columbia River Slough, southeast of St. Johns, and began building one of the largest meatpacking plants in the world; it dwarfed the 600-acre Union Stockyards in Chicago, made infamous by Upton Sinclair's 1906 exposé, *The Jungle*. In its 1914 *Book of the Stockyards,* Swift described the North Portland Union Stock Yards as "a great live stock market, covering many acres with railroad tracks, pens, unloading docks, buildings and other facilities adequate to the transaction of an enormous daily business." In 1913,

the plant processed 30,000 cows, hogs, sheep, and horses every day, handled by an army of 1,500 workers. As it had in other cities, Swift & Company bought up land around the stockyards and built a company town, which it named Kenton, thoughtfully sited due south of the plant because "the prevailing wind tends to blow downriver away from the home section thus dispelling and dissipating disagreeable odors attendant with its operation."

In addition to hundreds of wood-framed bungalows for laborers—and much larger

cement-block mansions for executives that lined the company's town main street, Denver Avenue—Swift built a hotel for visiting cattlemen, a bank, a firehouse, a school, and a "Stockyard Express" trolley. Although Swift closed the yards in the 1950s, Kenton retains its image as a working class community, at least in spirit, via a three-story statue of Paul Bunyan. Standing at the intersection of Denver and Interstate avenues, it was built in 1959 to greet visitors to Oregon's centennial celebration, held on the grounds of the former Swift livestock pavilion.

Sprawling over 3,400 acres on the outskirts of Kenton, Portland's Union Stockyards were more than five times bigger than Chicago's infamous Union Stockyards. Workers, photographed in 1911, inspect some of the 4,000 head of cattle that moved through the yards each day.

The intersection of North Denver and Lombard, at the southern edge of Kenton, bustles in the 1940s. For another decade, the Kenton neighborhood would remain a company town that revolved largely around the goings-on of the Union Stockyards, which left town in the 1950s. Here, a diesel bus has already displaced the Swift & Company's "Stockyard Express" trolley.

In 1959, Kenton-area businesses erected a 30-foot-tall statue of Paul Bunyan to welcome the eight million visitors expected for Oregon's Centennial Exposition. The Centennial Exposition, which was held on the grounds of the former livestock pavilion (now the Portland Expo Center) just outside of Kenton, was the largest fair held on the West Coast since San Francisco's World's Fair of 1939. In February 2009, Kenton's six-ton Paul Bunyan statue became the only roadside attraction in Oregon to be placed on the National Register of Historical Places, honored as "a well-crafted example of roadside architecture."

# THE EXPO CENTER

Swift & Company and other investors built the Pacific International Exposition Center in the early 1900s to accommodate the largest livestock trade show on the West Coast. In May 1942, the U.S. military commandeered the facility and turned it into the Portland Assembly Center, a temporary holding area for 3,500 Portland residents of Japanese ancestry. They lived in hastily constructed plywood apartments erected on a platform over the dirt floor while permanent internment camps were built in Idaho, California, and Wyoming. George Katagiri, a retired Portland elementary school teacher, was 16 years old when he, his parents, and his two older sisters were forced to leave their home near Southeast Hawthorne Boulevard and relocate to the camp.

"The Assembly Center was like a small city, with a security department, a fire department, a recreation hall, and a school, although there weren't any desks or books," an 82-year-old Katagiri recalled in 2008.

As quickly as it was built, the internment camp was disassembled and the pavilion reverted to its former use. After Kenton's Union Stockyards closed in the 1950s, Multnomah County acquired the hall and rechristened it as the Expo Center, a venue for trade shows and the annual county fair. Today, the only reminder of the Expo Center's incarnation as the Portland Assembly Center is a memorial at the facility's light rail station: a Japanese-style timber gateway festooned with hundreds of steel replicas of internee identification tags that glitter in the breeze wafting off the nearby Columbia River.

This 1919 poster advertised the Pacific International Livestock Exposition, an annual show hosted by Swift & Company and other meatpacking plants that did business in the North Portland area.

Internees arrive for processing at the Pacific International Exposition Center. From May through October 1942, it was known as the Portland Assembly Center, a temporary staging area where Portlanders of Japanese descent were housed before being sent to permanent internment camps in Idaho, California, and Wyoming.

Image cropped

## Memorial to Japanese Internment

At the Expo Center light rail station—the end of North Portland's Yellow Line—a timber-framed gateway *(right)* is strung with steel replicas of identification tags issued to those who were being relocated to internment camps, memorializing a dark period from the Expo Center's past. Also incorporated into the piece are excerpts from newspaper articles, a livestock pavilion blueprint, and a copy of the exclusion order *(left)* directing Portlanders of Japanese ancestry to the Portland Assembly Center.

# VANPORT

Just like it raced Liberty Ships through production, Henry Kaiser's ship-building company built housing for its workers at breakneck speed during the latter half of 1942. In just four and a half months, the company threw up a city of prefabricated apartment houses that were built on a floodplain 15 feet below grade, near the confluence of the Willamette and Columbia rivers, just north of present-day Kenton. At its height, Vanport boasted 32,000 residents, and Kaiser billed it as the world's largest war-housing community. It was Oregon's second-largest city, containing 9,942 apartments (renting for $28 a month, which is $365 present-day), 24-hour nurseries, a hospital, a movie theater, and three fire stations.

To the group of people, predominently African American, who remained in Kaiser's instant city three years after the shipyards closed on May 30, 1948, Vanport resembled a scene straight from the Great Flood. At 5 P.M., the Columbia River, supercharged with snowmelt, burst through the earthen berm that held back the river, sending a ten-foot wave of water that literally wiped Vanport off the map, sweeping buildings off their foundations, drowning 15, and leaving 18,700 homeless. Today, what was once Oregon's second-largest city (now the home of Heron Lakes Golf Course and the Portland International Raceway) has disappeared without much of a trace, save for an art installation at the Delta Park/Vanport light rail station.

By mid-October 1942, more than 2,000 workers were employed at the site, now dubbed Kaiserville. "13,000 men and women were hired before its completion with a maximum of about 5,000 working at any one time," writes Manly Maben in *Vanport,* his 1987 history of North Portland's short-lived instant city. "Because the buildings were deemed temporary they were not only constructed of wood, but were set on wood foundations, which, fortunately, enabled them to float like corks during the later flood."

On May 30, 1948, a flood-swollen Columbia River broke through an earthen berm and inundated the city of Vanport, which was built on a below-grade floodplain just north of Kenton. Although many of Vanport's residents had moved away when the shipyards closed after the war, 18,700 were left with nowhere to live. Here, flood victims and rescuers join hands to reach higher ground.

### Delta Park

The city-owned Portland International Raceway *(above center)* was built atop the ruins of the City of Vanport. The U.S. Army Corps of Engineers sold the site to the city in 1960, which paved over the memory of Vanport with an asphalt racetrack, a venue for the first Rose Festival auto races; the inaugural Rose Cup race was held here in June 1961. And at the Delta Park/Vanport light rail station *(right)*, steel sculptures by artist Linda Wysong recall the rooftops of Vanport apartment houses, which, submerged up to their rafters, floated off their foundations during the Flood of 1948 that wiped the mammoth housing project off the map.

In the 1980s, Kurt and Rob Widmer redeveloped the block at North Interstate Avenue and North Russell Street as Widmer Brothers Brewery, the largest brewery in Oregon. The former Interstate Tavern, shown here in the foreground in the 1940s, is now occupied by the brewery's German-themed restaurant, The Gasthaus Pub.

# INTERSTATE AVENUE

Before the Portland section of Interstate 5 was completed in 1964, north- and south-bound automobile through-traffic traveled along Interstate Avenue, a vestigial highway that parallels I-5 three blocks west from the Steel Bridge on the Willamette River to the Columbia Slough at Kenton. In 2004, the Interstate MAX Yellow Line, a north-south extension of the city's light rail system, was shunted up the middle of the former freeway. Now trains come and go every 15 minutes, following the route of the old highway through the industrial and residential heart of old Albina. After crossing the Willamette from downtown, Interstate MAX trains stop at the Rose Garden Arena across from cargo ships unloading grain at an elevator on the waterfront, and then at the Albina/Mississippi station where tractor trailers

loaded with shipping containers rumble into and out of Union Pacific's 19th century freight yard.

From the Albina Yards, light rail trains climb to the summit of the bluff; continue through the Overlook neighborhood; pass neon-lit, 1950s-era motor lodges; go through the former meatpacking town of Kenton; and end at the Expo Center—the livestock pavilion turned exhibition hall at the very tip of North Portland. Once the new multibillion-dollar Interstate Bridge is completed—expected within the next decade—the Yellow Line will cross the Columbia to the city of Vancouver, Washington, traveling from North Portland's past, and into the future.

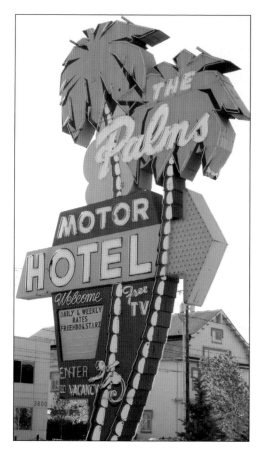

This animated neon sign outside The Palms motel in North Portland's Overlook neighborhood dates from 1949. Today, the city wants to designate the mile-long stretch of Interstate Avenue from North Overlook Boulevard to North Killingsworth Street as a historic neon district. It would preserve the avenue's Las Vegas–style signage as vestigial businesses dating from the strip's highway heyday are redeveloped into condominiums that cater to commuters on the MAX light rail line down the middle of North Portland's rendition of Route 66.

A downtown-bound Interstate MAX light rail train leaves the Albina/Mississippi station.

## THE ALIBI

As legend has it, the Alibi, one of the most storied of the many watering holes on North Interstate Avenue, dates back to the late 1800s, when it was known as the Chat 'n' Nibble, a roadhouse along a dirt thoroughfare rutted from wagon wheels. With the advent of the automobile (and pavement), the Chat 'n' Nibble was reincarnated as Max's Alibi until the property changed hands in the late 1940s, when its name was truncated, and the watering hole was reinvented as a tiki bar. Inside, the bamboo and thatch-themed lounge looks and feels much as it did during Truman's presidency, when unemployed workers from shuttered shipyards on Swan Island and St. Johns hoisted Mai Tais, and the talk of the town was how Columbia River floodwaters had wiped out the last vestige of Henry Kaiser's Portland empire—the ill-fated City of Vanport just a few miles up the road. *Shots of Portland* author David Richardson describes the bar as "Dark, tropical, and impeccably decorated in the Polynesian fashion."

After returning to Portland from Hawaii in the late 1940s, barkeep Roy Ell bought the property and gave the watering hole its distinctive Trader Vic's–style decor, which hasn't changed much since.

# PORTLAND POLONIA

In 1907, Polish immigrants who worked on the docks and in railyards along Albina's waterfront pooled paychecks and labor and began building St. Stanislaus Church at the corner of North Failing Street (named for Portland pioneer and former mayor Henry Failing) and Interstate Avenue (formerly Patton Avenue) in Overlook, then a mostly Slavic-speaking blue collar enclave on the bluff overlooking the Albina Yards. Archbishop Alexander Christie—who, in 1901, founded the University of Portland one neighborhood over—celebrated the first mass here on December 6, 1908. The simple one-story, wood-framed sanctuary, the first Polish church in Oregon, remains the only Catholic church in Oregon that offers a Polish-language mass. Also, only Polish-speaking pastors have lived in the St. Stanislaus rectory, with the lone exception of the 1960s, when Poles began leaving the neighborhood in droves after Interstate 5 was built in the church's backyard. In 1911, opposite the church, parishioners built Polonia Hall, a Polish community center with a vast hardwood dance floor, a kitchen staffed by pierogie-making *babushka*, and a library stocked with Polish newspapers, magazines, and books.

St. Stanislaus was designated a historical landmark by the city of Portland in September 1993. To celebrate the occasion, the following October, St. Stanislaus held its first Polish Festival; every autumn it draws thousands to Polonia Hall for polka dancing and feasting on comfort foods like *galabki* (cabbage rolls) and *kielbasa i bigos* (sausage and hunter's stew). Such fare can also be found at Grandpa's Café, the parish's cozy basement restaurant, open only on Friday evenings and Sundays after the 11 o'clock Polish mass, when Zywiec beer—and Polish conversation—flows freely.

A folk troupe dances onstage outside St. Stanislaus Church at the parish's annual Polish festival.

*Above:* Polish immigrant parishoners of St. Stanislaus Roman Catholic Church pose on the steps of the newly completed sanctuary they built with their own hands in 1907.

## Polish Festival

A polka band *(above)* and children in traditional costume *(left)* perform at St. Stanislaus Church's annual Polish Festival, the largest event of its kind in the Northwest. It draws more than 10,000 pierogi-loving and polka-dancing revelers at the end of every September. In 2008, festival-goers consumed more than 15,000 dumplings and 6,000 bottles of imported Polish beer.

# NORTH WILLIAMS AVENUE

Before Portland annexed the City of Albina in 1891, Williams Avenue—located between Patton (present-day Interstate Avenue) and Union (present-day Martin Luther King Jr. Blvd.) avenues—served as the Main Street of the former city. The heart of Albina's business district was a distinctive commercial building with an onion-dome turret called the Hill Block Building, which Albina's first mayor, Charles H. Hill, built at the corner of Williams and Russell Street in 1890.

After the flood of 1948 destroyed Vanport, displaced African American shipyard workers settled in Albina in frame houses along North Williams Avenue, and the Hill Block Building became the center of the city's African American business district. Successive "urban renewal" projects (beginning with the construction of Memorial Coliseum south of North Russell Street in the late 1950s, then Interstate 5 in the late 1960s) fragmented Albina's African American community with condemnation of scores of dilapidated homes. The final blow came in 1969, when Emanuel Hospital tore down the Hill Block Building as part of a proposed 19-acre expansion of its campus. After protests from the African American community, the hospital lost federal funding for its expansion, and the site of the former Hill Block Building was paved over as a parking lot. But there was one concession: In 1978, the city used the onion dome, bricks, and other materials salvaged from the Hill Block Building to build a gazebo in nearby Dawson Park.

In 2008, North Williams Avenue reclaimed its status as a commercial district. Up the street from the former Hill Block Building, developers rehabbed a 30,000-square-foot former Oregon food bank warehouse into The Hub, a sprawling development with upscale businesses. It and several developments have accelerated the gentrification pushing Albina's African American community to more affordable—and less desirable—real estate along the East Side's easternmost fringes.

On January 27, 1907, an ice storm paralyzed Portland, downing trolley wires and knocking out the city's public transportation system, resulting in two equine fatalities on North Williams Avenue: The team that pulled the milk wagon pictured here was electrocuted when the wires fell.

The Hub includes a specialty coffee roaster, a yoga studio, a German toy store, a cooking school, an oyster bar, and a posh white-tablecloth restaurant.

Image cropped

## *Dawson Park Onion Dome*

With its distinctive onion dome turret, the 1892 Hill Block Building at North Williams Avenue and North Russell Street, shown here around the turn of the century *(top)*, was built by Albina's first mayor, Charles H. Hill. It served as the commercial hub of the neighborhood's once-thriving African American community but was razed in the 1970s to make room for an Emanuel Hospital expansion that was never realized. In July 2008, the city dedicated a renovated gazebo *(bottom)*, built with bricks and timbers and the iconic onion dome salvaged from the Hill Block Building.
It serves as the centerpiece of North Portland's Dawson Park.

Kennedy Elementary School students dance around the maypole during May Day festivities in 1916. The school, which is now a brewpub, was named after John D. Kennedy, the pioneer who homesteaded the tract.

# KENNEDY SCHOOL

Kennedy Elementary School was named not for John F. Kennedy but for John D. Kennedy, an Irishman who emigrated to San Francisco as a 15-year-old in 1866. In the 1880s, Kennedy relocated to East Portland, purchased a large tract of farmland along present-day Northeast 33rd Avenue, and built a house and outbuildings near present-day Simpson Street.

In 1890, Kennedy subdivided his farm as Kennedy's Addition and tried to sell off lots to the waves of newcomers expected to throng the area after the 1891 annexation of East Portland, but his property's remote location (two blocks east of the nearest streetcar line) and

the financial panic of 1893 scuttled his plans. Kennedy's Addition sat undeveloped a decade after the turn of the century, when short on cash and hoping to attract families with children to the area, Kennedy sold off the barn, chicken coop, and orchards on the four acres behind his house to the Portland School District for an elementary school.

The Kennedy School was designed by the school district's architect Floyd A. Naramore and inspired by a fire that gutted a multistory public school in Ohio. It was deemed "groundbreaking" when it opened in 1915, and in 1916, *Ladies Home Journal* touted it as the "First One-Story School of Its Kind in

the Nation." Sixty years later, faced with declining enrollment and a deteriorating building, the school district planned to demolish Kennedy School. However, a coalition headed by John D. Kennedy's daughter and a historic preservationist living in the old Kennedy farmstead warded off the wrecking ball until pub magnates Mike and Brian McMenamin purchased the property in 1994. After a three-year renovation, it reopened as McMenamins Kennedy School, an inn where the principal's office serves as the front desk, the guest rooms are converted classrooms (complete with blackboards), and the brewpub has themed bars such as the Detention Room.

The school's reincarnation ignited interest and reinvestment in nearby Northeast Alberta Avenue, a long-neglected, crime-plagued commercial strip. Artists spruced up the storefronts, and the Alberta Arts District (as the area is now known) attracts throngs to open houses at galleries, restaurants, and other art spaces on the last Thursday of each month. The Kennedy School is the most popular gallery of them all. Murals by local artists depict the school's history, and the school's walls are covered with friezes that include four bas-relief reproductions of 15th-century Florentine masterpieces that John D. Kennedy commissioned and donated to the school in 1916.

## McMenamins Kennedy School

In 1997, local brewpub impresarios Mike and Brian McMenamin put a decidedly Portland twist on the concept of adaptive reuse of buildings. They transformed the historic Kennedy Elementary School—which closed in 1974 due to falling enrollment—into a schoolhouse-themed brewpub that includes a leafy beer garden *(upper left)* and a boutique inn. In addition to registered hotel guests, residents from the Alberta neighborhood are allowed to use the inn's soaking pool *(above)* at their leisure. Inside the re-imagined Kennedy School, classrooms have been converted into hotel rooms (some complete with original slate blackboards), while the Detention Room *(left)* now caters to whiskey-swilling cigar aficionados.

# LAURELHURST

In 1869, William Sargent Ladd purchased Hazelwood, a 486-acre farm (bounded by present-day Northeast Halsey and Southeast Stark streets between 29th and 44th avenues) as an investment property, reasoning that once a bridge to East Portland was built, the value of the acreage would increase exponentially as the East Side opened to residential development. While he waited for the bridge, and prospective homebuyers, Ladd converted Hazelwood into a showcase ranch he renamed Hazel Fern. Herds of purebred Jersey and Guernsey cows, Clydesdale draft horses, and Cotswold sheep grazed the rolling meadows of alfalfa and clover and watered from a bucolic pond that children in the area used as a swimming hole. Ladd himself died during the Panic of 1893, which cooled the East Side's once-hot real estate market for another 15 years. His three sons formed Ladd Estate Company and sold off Hazel Fern to the Seattle-based Laurelhurst Company for $2 million ($47 million today), then the largest real estate transaction in Portland's history.

The Laurelhurst Company platted nearly 3,000 lots for homes, which deed restrictions mandated must cost at least $3,000. They also banned apartments and hotels (along with Chinese, Japanese, and African Americans) from the gated community, named Laurelhurst after an enclave of manor homes the company developed in Seattle. The company hired landscape designer John C. Olmsted (an investor) to plat the subdivision, and similar to Ladd's Addition, a roundabout was placed at its very center. They also sold 32 acres to the city for an Olmsted-designed public park and deeded the right-of-way along Northeast Glisan Street to the Portland Railway, Light and Power Company, which built the Montavilla streetcar line to service the subdivision. The line was critical to the subdivision's success, depositing prospective homebuyers at a real estate office in the center of the roundabout. One of the first buyers was influential *Oregonian* editor Harvey Scott, who erected a mansion on a corner lot across from the roundabout; other elites quickly followed. After the last lots were sold in the 1920s, the real estate office was torn down and replaced with a gilded statue of Joan of Arc astride a steed that Ladd himself would have admired.

Ice skaters cavort on Laurelhurst Park's frozen Firwood Lake in the winter of 1917, three years after Portland Parks superintendent Emanuel Mische finished landscaping the 32-acre crown jewel of the posh Laurelhurst subdivision (seen rising on the park's perimeter in the background).

During the 1920s and 1930s, the queen of the Portland Rose Festival was crowned on a barge that floated on Laurelhurst's Firwood Lake; pictured here is Rachel Atkinson (flanked by pint-size attendants), who was crowned on Firwood Lake in June 1931.

*Above:* Soon after relocating from New York City to open a private practice in Portland in 1924, architect Herman Brookman, one of Portland's most prolific residential architects during the first half of the 20th century, designed this rambling Mediterranean-style home fronting Laurelhurst Park. "On a beautiful site overlooking Laurelhurst Park, the seventeen-room house shows Brookman's mastery of the architectural form," wrote William J. Harkins and William F. Willingham in *Classic Houses of Portland, Oregon 1850–1950.* "With the sculptural richness of the façade on one side, the beauty of Laurelhurst Park on the other, and the luxury of the formal gardens of the parterre in between, the private and intimate space is one of the most attractive in the city."

*Left:* After the Laurelhurst Company sold off the last lots of its Laurelhurst subdivision in the 1920s, a sales office in the center of the neighborhood was torn down and replaced with something more appropriate: a gilded Joan of Arc statue, the gift of physician Waldo Henry Coe, who wanted to memorialize the fallen soldiers of World War I.

## LAURELHURST PARK

OLMSTED BROTHERS HORTICULTURALIST Emanuel Mische, who worked as Portland's public parks superintendent from 1908 to 1914, landscaped 26.8-acre Laurelhurst Park using a plan sketched by John Charles Olmsted. Like New York City's Central Park, Olmsted segregated Laurelhurst into zones by designated activity, including a picnic grove, a rhododendron garden, a children's lawn, a play park, and as its centerpiece, a former livestock watering pond/swimming hole that Mische enlarged to three acres and rechristened Firwood Lake. From 1921 to 1931, Firwood Lake was the site of the Rose Festival queen's coronation, which took place on a flotilla of ornately decorated barges. The lake also attracted hundreds of ducks, geese, and swans, some of which are shown below, patroling the lake in 1920. Two swans became infamous for their antics: A militant swan named General Pershing chased park users away from the water's edge, and Big Boy, a more welcoming swan, was taught by a parkgoer to greet visitors with a nod of its head and a double honk that sounded like "hello."

In January 1898, a regiment of Oregon National Guard troops gathered at Camp McKinley. It was a horse-racing track in Irvington (the site of present-day Irving Park) that, during the Spanish-American War, had been commandeered as a mustering point for soldiers leaving to fight in the Philippines.

# IRVINGTON

In 1852, a Scotland-born mariner named William Irving filed a donation claim for a 640-acre tract now known as Irvington (bounded on the north and south by present-day Fremont and Halsey streets between 7th and 24th avenues). However, he left to pursue his fortune in the gold fields along the Fraser River in British Columbia, where he died in 1872. Except for a dirt horse track on the site of present-day Irving Park during the late 19th and early 20th centuries, Irving's land attracted scant attention from developers until 1907, when the F. B. Holbrook Company began marketing "Irvington Park" as "a private residence park" for middle- and upper-class professionals. Like nearby Laurelhurst, deed restrictions required property owners to build residences that cost at least $2,500 and added amenities like asphalt streets and concrete sidewalks; sewer, water, and gas mains; and curbs fitted with steel hitching rings to secure the teams of visiting guests.

Opportunists like Holbrook and the Prospect Park Company (which subdivided a 28-block parcel between Northeast Knott and Siskiyou, from Northeast 7th to 14th avenues as an upper-class residential community) carved up Irving's claim and built hundreds of Craftsman style bungalows, along with a few mansions. During the Great Depression, future librarian and writer Beverly Cleary spent her teenage years in a "comfortable and artistic" Irvington home off Northeast Klickitat Street, which became the setting of her best-selling *Ramona Quimby* children's books.

*Left:* In 1905, Gustav Freiwald, proprietor of Star Brewery and St. Elmo Hotel in Vancouver, Washington, hired residential architect Emil Schacht to design a mansion at the corner of Northeast 15th Avenue and Weidler Street. Freiwald rejected Schacht's renderings, hiring unknown H. H. Menges to embellish Schacht's original Craftsman concept with ornate Queen Anne flourishes. After Freiwald's heirs sold the home in 1938, it served as a boarding house and apartment complex until 1992, when it was renovated as the Lion and the Rose Victorian Bed & Breakfast Inn.

### *Beverly Cleary*

Northeast Klickitat Street *(above)* is the setting of *Ramona the Pest* and other beloved children's books by author Beverly Cleary, who lived in the Irvington neighborhood as a teenager in the late 1920s and early 1930s. During summer months, children splash in fountains that spurt from the ground near the bronze statues of fictional heroine Ramona Quimby and dog Ribsy at the Beverly Clearly Sculpture Garden *(right)*, which is located in Grant Park, four blocks from the real Northeast Klickitat Street.

# LLOYD DISTRICT

When Portland mayor Terry Shrunk cut the ribbon at Lloyd Center on August 1, 1960, and told a crowd of 5,000 to let the shopping begin, he borrowed a page from the Benson Hotel (which sent homing pigeons aloft at its grand opening in 1913). *TIME* magazine recounted that "to the blare of bands and the fluttering of banners, 700 pigeons winged into the sky over Portland, Ore…to carry the good news to 29 Oregon and Washington cities." Lloyd Center was feted as the largest mall in America—it had been a long time coming.

Southern California oil baron Ralph Bramel Lloyd began buying real estate along present-day Northeast Multnomah Street at the southern edge of Irvington in 1925, after finding a gusher on the family's ranch in Ventura. He was intent on building a self-contained city-within-a-city to spur economic development on the East Side. By 1929, Lloyd had acquired more than 800 lots. He began building a hotel, but the onset of the Great Depression halted construction, and World War II only delayed the project further. When Lloyd died in 1953, his four daughters formed the Lloyd Corporation and secured the financing and permits they needed to realize their father's dream.

For decades, Lloyd Center thrived. The skating rink attracted a visit by Robert Kennedy and his family during a campaign stop in 1968; in 1973, the future Olympic figure-skating star and drama queen, Tonya Harding, took her first lap around the ice as a three-year-old. But as others copied Lloyd's idea and mall culture took root, Lloyd Center began to look dated and started to decline. A 1990 update enclosed the mall, which today looks no different than any other mall in America but retains the bragging rights of being the first—and remains the biggest—in the state of Oregon.

One of the most defining physical features of the Lloyd District is Sullivan's Gulch, pictured here circa 1915, a vast east-west oriented depression named for Irish pioneer Timothy Sullivan. Today, light rail tracks follow the path of Sullivan's Gulch to and from Portland International Airport and Gresham.

The nearly completed Lloyd Center is visible in the background beyond the Douglas fir trees of Holladay Park (named for stagecoach tycoon Ben Holladay, who owned the tract in the late 19th century, when the area was known as Holladay's Addition). When Lloyd Center opened in 1960, it was the largest shopping mall in America.

## Oregon Convention Center

Completed in 1990, the million-square-foot Oregon Convention Center *(below)* is the largest exhibition hall in Oregon; the center's 34,200-square-foot Grand Portland Ballroom is also the largest ballroom in the city. The center's twin glass spires *(right)*, at 260 feet tall, reflect the sunrise and sunset, making the building the most visible structure on the city's East Side; they also channel daylight into the center of the building. To clean all 1,500 panes of glass, window washers climb a vertical ladder inside each tower, open a hatch, and rappel over the edge toting squeegees and buckets. When the aircraft warning beacons at the tip of the needlelike antennas burn out, the same daredevils scale the spires to switch out the bulbs by hand.

# MEMORIAL COLISEUM/ ROSE GARDEN ARENA

In 1954, Portland voters approved an $8-million bond measure for the construction of an auditorium on 30 acres of crumbling East Side waterfront (then home to a sizable percentage of the city's African American population) between the Broadway and Steel bridges that would be dedicated to Oregon's veterans. When it opened for business on November 1, 1960, Memorial Coliseum, designed by Chicago-based Skidmore, Owings & Merrill, was hailed as a masterpiece. Nobody had ever seen anything quite like it—a steel and glass Modernist cube with a concrete bowl of an amphitheater at its center, shrouded by floor-to-ceiling curtains that, when lowered, revealed a stunning backdrop of downtown Portland's cityscape gleaming across the water.

In 1970, Memorial Coliseum became the home court of the city's new NBA franchise: the Portland Trail Blazers. Known as "The Glass Palace," the Trail Blazers' 13,000-seat home court earned a reputation as one of the loudest arenas in the league. This vibrant venue set the stage for the Trail Blazers' ascendance in 1977 to its first—and thus far only—NBA title, attracting sell-out crowds and interest from Seattle-based Microsoft billionaire Paul Allen, who acquired the team—and the Coliseum—in 1988.

After the Blazers made the NBA Finals in 1990 and again in 1992, to accommodate Portland's "Blazermania" (from 1977 to 1995, the Coliseum would host 810 consecutive sellout home games)— and maximize his profits—Allen built the Rose Garden Arena, a much larger and more conventional stadium, on one of Memorial Coliseum's parking lots. When the $262-million Rose Garden Arena—an unremarkable (some call it soulless) concrete hat box designed by Kansas city mega-stadium architect Ellerbe Becket—opened in 1995, the Blazers entered a tailspin from which the team has only recently begun to recover. With one of the worst records in the league (as well as lackluster attendance) through most of the last decade, Allen's Oregon Arena Corp filed for bankruptcy in 2004. Even though Allen has invested much of his fortune, including $2 million on an "acoustical cloud" mechanical sound system meant to mimic the roar of the Glass Palace next door, he's never been able to recapture the magic of Memorial Coliseum, which sits all but abandoned to the north, facing an uncertain future. Many feel it's only a matter of time before Memorial Coliseum goes the way of the Seattle Kingdome and the distinguished building's curtain falls a final time with a dramatic implosion.

Portland Trail Blazer LaRue Martin, who joined the team in 1972 as the NBA's number one draft pick, takes command of his home court during a 1972 face off with the Lakers at Memorial Coliseum. The Trail Blazers, Portland's only major league franchise (until the Portland Timbers join Major League Soccer in 2011), entered the NBA in 1970.

Portland Trail Blazers coach Jack Ramsay gets a hero's welcome with a downtown parade on Broadway after the Blazers won the 1977 NBA Championship, the team's only NBA title.

In 1970, Memorial Coliseum *(above)* became the 13,000-seat home court of the Portland Trail Blazers, earning a reputation as one of the loudest arenas in the league. Ever since the Blazers relocated to the nearby Rose Garden Arena *(right)* in 1995, this vibrant venue has faced an uncertain future. In 2009, after Portland Timbers owner Merritt Paulson announced plans to renovate PGE Park as a Major League Soccer venue, Portland's mayor agreed to replace the Coliseum with a baseball stadium for Paulson's minor league team, the Portland Beavers. After a firestorm of protests from preservationists who vowed to save the Glass Palace, the mayor proposed an alternative venue for the project.

# THE GROTTO

Father Ambrose Mayer was a Catholic priest from the Servite Friars (a monastic order founded in Florence, Italy, in 1233) who had relocated to Portland at the invitation of Archbishop Alexander Christie. In 1923, Mayer received the archbishop's blessing to transform a 62-acre parcel of cliff-top land (off of Northeast Sandy Boulevard and Northeast 82nd Avenue in the Parkrose neighborhood near present-day Portland International Airport) into a shrine and botanical garden known as the National Sanctuary of Our Sorrowful Mother.

Mayer described the site as "a mess of almost impenetrable undergrowth, fallen rocks, thickets and debris," but he quickly went to work, building an open-air cathedral for as many as 30,000 worshippers. It was buttressed with towering firs and faced a grotto hewn into the base of the basalt cliff face, with an altar lit by twin torch-bearing seraphim and crowned by a Carrera marble replica of Michelangelo's *Pieta* (a statue of Mary bearing the crucified body of Christ that sits at the entrance of Saint Peter's Basilica at the Vatican in Rome). Ten years after founding The Grotto, Mayer was dispatched to other Servite sites around the world. He returned in 1970 to a sanctuary transformed with lushly landscaped gardens, two chapels, a monastery, and an elevator for transporting pilgrims more than 100 feet up the cliff to view a 2,600-pound statue of Mary selected by the Pope to celebrate the 700th Anniversary of the Servites. The sanctuary's founder died a few months after his homecoming and was buried in a simple grave atop the cliff.

Worshippers in 1954 pay their respects at the National Sanctuary of Our Sorrowful Mother's grotto, an altar carved into a basalt cliff face that's crowned with a replica of Michelangelo's *Pieta*. The sanctuary, known as The Grotto, is a 62-acre Catholic shrine on a bluff in Northeast Portland's Parkrose neighborhood that was established in 1923 by the Servite Friars.

Monks at The Grotto built this simple chapel for the 1934 Marian Congress, a religious conference attended by 60,000 Catholic church officials and worshippers from around the world, including Cardinal Alexis Henry Lépicier, a papal representative from Rome.

The Grotto's 500-seat Chapel of Mary is decorated for the Festival of Lights—one of the city's most popular Christmas events that typically draws crowds of 50,000 or more.

Arriving in Portland on September 14, 1927, after flying solo across the continent, Charles Lindbergh taxis the *Spirit of St. Louis,* one of the first planes to land on the grass runway at Portland's first municipal airport on Swan Island. Newspapers celebrated its moment in Lindy's limelight with triumphant illustrations, such as the editorial cartoon at left from *The Portland Telegram.*

# PORTLAND INTERNATIONAL AIRPORT

Aviator Charles Lindbergh electrified the city when he flew across the continent in the *Spirit of St. Louis* and landed at Portland's first municipal airport, then located on Swan Island, touching down a minute ahead of schedule at 1:59 P.M. on September 14, 1927.

Adulatory multitudes never had a chance to swarm the *Spirit of St. Louis* once it taxied to a stop, however, because the airport—yet to be completed—lacked a bridge to the mainland; the hero had to be ferried across the Willamette in department store magnate (and future Oregon governor) Julius Meier's yacht for an official tickertape parade.

Not long after the airport's completion on February 1, 1931, *The Oregonian* toured the facility's single-gate passenger terminal (serviced by two 12-passenger trimotor planes per day) and deemed it "among the first 14 finest" in the United States.

Unfortunately, Swan Island Airport was obsolete by 1936, its runway unable to accommodate ever-larger passenger planes. Thus, that year, the Port of Portland purchased 700 acres along the Columbia River at the airport's present location and began building a "Super Port." Columbia-Portland Airport was completed four years later and then expanded in 1958. It reopened as

Portland International Airport, with an extended 8,800-foot runway—the large new jets taxied into a futuristic terminal with arrivals and departures gates for 18 airliners. The airport's souvenir pamphlet "New Portland International Airport Welcomes the Jet Age," noted amenities like 19 gateside roomettes equipped with beds, showers, and telephones. After several more expansions and upgrades, PDX (as it's known to locals, who prefer to use the official FAA designation) may be the nation's 31st busiest in terms of takeoffs and landings, but it's tops in terms of passenger satisfaction: In 2008, readers of *Conde Nast Traveler* voted PDX the nation's best airport for a third consecutive year.

One of Portland International Airport's most striking architectural features is as practical as it is beautiful. In 2000, a 100,000 square-foot glass canopy was erected over the arrivals and departures gates to shield passengers from Portland's ever-present rain. The firm that designed the structure, Zimmer Gunsul Frasca Partnership, also designed the city's other signature glass embellishment: the twin towers atop the Oregon Convention Center.

This ultramodern, yet cozy, lobby lounge awaits jet-lagged guests at Aloft, a boutique airport hotel that represents a departure from the 19 gateside roomettes the airport offered travelers after its last major remodel in 1958.

# OTHER RIVER CITIES

In 1828, a 44-year-old French-speaking, Quebec-born physician named Jean-Baptiste McLoughlin paddled a canoe past the mouth of the Clackamas River (where a 300-foot-long longhouse served as headquarters of the Clackamas Nation) and gaped at the awesome spectacle of the roaring *Tumwater*, deeming it "the most important place in this country."

As head ("chief factor") of the Hudson's Bay Company trading post at Fort Vancouver on the Columbia—not far from the Willamette's mouth 15 miles downriver—McLoughlin was the most powerful figure in all of Oregon Country, governing a region of unbroken wilderness that stretched from the Rockies to the Pacific, between present-day California and Alaska.

A year later, McLoughlin claimed the falls for the Hudson's Bay Company, building three log cabins on an island at the base of the thundering cascade. Native Americans burned the cabins to the ground. In 1832, he dynamited a mill out of basalt on the island and built a house and store with lumber squared at the site. To solidify HBC's claim,

McLoughlin built a homestead, then hired a surveyor to plat 640 acres on the east bank from the falls to the mouth of the Clackamas River as a townsite that early settlers referred to as Willamette Falls. McLoughlin incorporated the site in 1844 as Oregon City, intending the settlement to be true to its name: the principal city of Oregon Country.

Oregon City became a national destination as the endpoint of the Oregon Trail with the opening of the Barlow Road in 1846—the first wagon road over the Cascades. As the trickle of settlers turned into a flood (more than 1,000 settlers in 145 wagons traveled the Barlow Road in its first year), the Oregon Treaty of 1846 ceded land south of the 49th Parallel to the United States, ending

In this 1900 image of downtown Oregon City, the commercial district sprawls from the foot of the bluffs to the river's edge. "The town has two weekly newspapers, a first-class theater, four hotels, three livery stables, three public and four lodge halls, and a large number of mercantile houses," boasted the *Oregon City Courier-Herald* on New Year's Day 1901, when the city of 6,000 was one-fifteenth the size of Portland. "These and the thousands of other unmentioned facts, make the future substantial growth of Oregon City as certain as Holy Writ."

*Left:* Established in 1829, Oregon City, on the right-hand side of the photo, is the oldest incorporated city west of the Mississippi.

Hudson's Bay Company's dominion over the region. McLoughlin, himself at odds with HBC (which censured him for aiding U.S. settlers with provisions from Fort Vancouver's stores) resigned his post in 1846 and retired to a two-story home in Oregon City, which in 1848, became the official capital of Oregon Territory (the fledgling state of Oregon). In addition to a statehouse, as the seat of the provisional government, Oregon City boasted the only federal land office west of the Mississippi where settlers could file claims.

## OREGON CITY TAKES A BACK SEAT

Nevertheless, many downstream upstarts challenged Oregon City's supremacy. Just down the east bank of the river was Milwaukie, founded in 1848 as Dogwood City by Lot Whitcomb, who two years later built the first steamboat on the Willamette. On the west bank, downstream from the falls, the town of Oswego, founded in 1847, was promoted as the Pittsburgh of the West with the discovery of iron in its hills. The founders of the fledgling downriver townsite of Portland were both residents of Oregon City: Francis Pettygrove ran a general store, and Asa Lovejoy, who had a law office in town, had been elected Oregon City's mayor in 1845 (the same year he lost the fateful coin toss to Pettygrove). Downriver from Portland was Linnton, and across the river from Linnton, St. Johns. Sauvie Island sat at the confluence of the Columbia and Willamette rivers. On the opposite bank of the Columbia—six miles upriver from the mouth of the Willamette—Fort Vancouver was once the stronghold of Oregon Country. There were many possibilities, but by 1850, none of these settlements held as much promise as Oregon City.

John McLoughlin

To legitimize his stake in Oregon City, McLoughlin renounced his British citizenship in 1849 and, after a two-year wait, was naturalized. By then it was too late: Under the Donation Land Law of 1850 (which granted acreage to U.S. citizens only), McLoughlin was forced to forfeit his claim, which was divvied up among American settlers. Stripped of his land, McLoughlin thumbed his nose at his enemies by becoming Oregon City's mayor in 1851. That same year, in a calculated move to undercut McLoughlin's influence, legislators voted to move the territory's capital from Oregon City to Salem; in 1853, the former statehouse became a hotel. John McLoughlin was still fighting to recover his land—and status—when he died in 1857. Two years later, Oregon became a state, and Portland, instead of Oregon City, became its most significant metropolis.

From 1818, until the Treaty of Oregon *(above)* was signed on June 15, 1846, the United States and Great Britain jointly occupied Oregon Country, the area west of the Rocky Mountains known today as the Pacific Northwest. Anticipating that the Columbia River would ultimately be renegotiated as the boundary between British and U.S. holdings, the Hudson's Bay Company established Fort Vancouver on the "British" (north) side of the Columbia, six miles upriver from the mouth of the Willamette, in 1824. That move staked Great Britain's claim to the territory north of the river, dominating commerce in the region for decades. The Treaty of Oregon, which established the boundary at the 49th parallel (the present-day border between the United States and Canada), marked the beginning of the decline of Fort Vancouver, which the Hudson's Bay Company relinquished to the U.S. Army in 1860.

On December 12, 1932, a rare freeze practically silenced the typically thundering Willamette Falls.

In 1849, the U.S. Army established an outpost on the bluff above Fort Vancouver and erected barracks for soldiers and officers, including future president Ulysses S. Grant, who was stationed there from 1852 to 1853.

# FORT VANCOUVER

Hudson's Bay Company established Fort Vancouver in 1824, siting its most far-flung trading post at Jolie Prairie, also known as Belle Vue Point, a shelf of land six miles upriver from the mouth of the Willamette, about 100 miles inland from the Pacific Ocean. The site was selected not for its *belle vue* but for its strategic position on the north bank of the Columbia River, which the British (who jointly occupied Oregon Country with the United States under the Treaty of 1818) anticipated to be the southernmost border of its territory. On March 18, 1825, George Simpson, the governor of the Columbia Department (as the British referred to Oregon Country) inspected the newly completed fort: a stockade of fir pickets with a double gate, warehouse, trading hall, and barracks encompassing less than an acre. He hoisted the Union Jack and wet its staff with a splash of Hudson's Bay rum, claiming the

fort he named after explorer George Vancouver for King George IV, then passed the bottle.

Aside from establishing the Crown's toehold in Oregon Country, the fort promised to be a commercial boon for the Hudson's Bay Company.

Native Americans and trappers came from every corner of Oregon Country to conduct business at the depot, which at its height in the mid-1840s had expanded into a walled city. The palisade itself was 20 feet tall and fenced nearly eight acres, including a bakery, chapel and rectory, bath house, blacksmith shop, schoolhouse, and hospital, as well as a home for the chief factor and a 16-room Bachelor's Range for subordinates. Outside the walls, a crude village sprawled across the plain. Known as Kanaka Town (for its plethora of Hawaiians) with a population of 600,

it was the largest settlement between present-day San Francisco and Sitka.

But the outpost was doomed. First, the fur market collapsed when fashion-fickle Londoners switched to top hats made of silk. Then in 1846, the Treaty of Oregon set the southern boundary of the British empire's Oregon Country holdings not at the Columbia River but at the 49th parallel—the present-day border with Canada. By 1860, Hudson's Bay Company had abandoned Fort Vancouver, and the U.S. Army took its place. Today, all that remains of the original fort (the stockade burned to the ground in 1866) is the name the British left behind: Vancouver—now a bedroom community of 162,000, a good many of whom jam the Interstate Bridge to Oregon on weekday mornings to seek their fortunes in Portland.

When this photograph was taken inside the Fort Vancouver palisade in May 1860, the Hudson's Bay Company had begun abandoning its trading post; shown here, left to right, are a warehouse, company store, bastion, granary, and office. The fort was officially vacated on June 14, 1860, when the Company's chief trader handed over the keys to the U.S. Army and sailed to Victoria aboard the *Otter*. The Army occupied the decrepit remains of Fort Vancouver for six years, until it was consumed by a fire; Philip H. Sheridan (who would later command the Union Army during the Civil War) had his wishes come true. According to the National Park Service's *History of Fort Vancouver and Its Physical Structure,* Sheridan had inspected the palisade and buildings in 1856 and deemed them "gloomy looking," declaring that it "would be a good thing if they would burn down."

Most of the Hudson's Bay Company employees who worked in Fort Vancouver lived in a village (depicted here, circa mid-19th century) that sprawled on the plain outside the fortress's western perimeter. With a population of 600 by the mid-1800s, it was known as Kanaka Town—*kanaka* is the Hawaiian word for "person."

Shown here in the 1890s, the City of Vancouver, Washington, was located within cannon shot of the fortress. It was incorporated in 1857, three years before the Hudson's Bay Company abandoned its claim to the area.

*Right:* Pictured here is the reconstructed bastion that stood in the northwest corner of the fort. The upper floor of the octagonal wooden turret housed a battery of eight "three-pounder" cannons, so-called because they fired cannonballs that weighed three pounds each.

*Above:* On October 8, 1929, the crew of a Russian monoplane named *The Land of the Soviets* created a sensation when they made an unscheduled stop at Pearson Field, an airstrip that was built to the east of the old fortress.

*Left:* The twin 18-pound cannons outside the chief factor's house (far right) inside the palisade of Fort Vancouver weren't functional but were meant to remind visitors of the British Empire's power over the region. The original home that John McLoughlin, Fort Vancouver's first chief factor, occupied was completed in 1836; McLoughlin would have used the raised area beneath the living quarters as a wine cellar.

A single span of the Interstate Bridge could handle the volume of traffic between Portland (background) and Vancouver in 1917; its twin was added in the 1950s. Today, it's notorious for bottlenecks; the bridge is scheduled for replacement by 2020.

This is a present-day view of downtown Vancouver, which locals refer to as "America's Vancouver."

## VANCOUVER LAND BRIDGE

ON AUGUST 23, 2008, NEW YORK ARTIST MAYA LIN (creator of the Washington, D.C., Vietnam Veterans Memorial) traveled to Fort Vancouver to dedicate the Vancouver Land Bridge (shown below), an earth-covered viaduct traversing the Lewis and Clark Highway that reconnects Jolie Plain with the long-disappeared Hudson's Bay Company wharf on the Columbia River. The $12.25 million bridge, designed by Seattle architect Johnpaul Jones, was the second major installation of Lin's Confluence Project, which retraces the final 450 miles of Meriwether Lewis and William Clark's journey down the Columbia River. Similar to the six other Lin-designed Confluence Project sites, the Fort Vancouver installation commemorates a stop along the explorers' route (the Corps of Discovery camped here on November 4, 1805), and compels visitors to reflect upon the impact subsequent settlement had on Native American culture. Diseases brought by Europeans at Fort Vancouver decimated an entire Chinookan village near the fort. By the 1830s, smallpox and other maladies had eliminated all but two percent of the Columbia Basin's Chinookan population.

# SAUVIE ISLAND

Since Lewis and Clark first happened upon this 26,000-acre island at the confluence of the Columbia and Willamette rivers, about the only thing that's changed has been its name. In 1805, explorer William Clark called it Wappato Island, after the potato-like tuber with arrowhead-shape leaves that was cultivated by the island's ancestral inhabitants, a band of 800 from the Multnomah nation. From 1834 to 1836, it was known as Wyeth Island for pioneer Nathaniel Wyeth, who operated a short-lived trading post called Fort William, which he abandoned after his plans to ship salmon and lumber to Hawaii failed to yield lucrative returns. Two years later, it became Sauvé's Island when the Hudson's Bay Company dispatched a French Canadian employee named Laurent Sauvé to tend 100 head of cattle on the island's western end. Sauvé managed the company's dairy herd for six years, retiring to a Willamette Valley farm in 1844, but the name stuck—first appearing on a map as Sauvie's Island in 1856, around the time it was carved up as donation claims by settlers from Portland. Since then, the island has remained all but frozen in time.

In 2000, Northwest Portland's island "neighborhood" (located ten miles downstream from downtown) was home to just 1,078 year-round residents, with a single general store, a post office, volunteer fire department, a school with four teachers and 90 students, and a few dozen dairy and vegetable farms. These farms serve as agriculture-themed amusement parks for city children on weekends in October. During this time, the island's population swells by several thousand toddlers, and pumpkin-laden cars try to cross the island's only bridge, creating a miles-long traffic jam that rivals rush hour on Interstate 5.

Seven miles of public beaches on the Columbia River attract swimmers and sunbathers to Sauvie Island during sun-soaked summer months.

On sunny weekends in October, thousands of Portlanders converge on Sauvie Island farm stands like these to tote pumpkins home for the holiday, jamming the typically tranquil island's two-lane roads.

During Halloween 2004, the Pumpkin Patch farm stand on Sauvie Island turned a corn field into a maze that, when seen from the air, formed a likeness of Sacajawea.

This Greek Revival home's original owner, James F. Bybee, was a horse breeder who relocated to Portland from Kentucky in the 1850s and claimed 640 acres on Sauvie Island. After living in the house for only a few years, Bybee sold the spread to physician Benjamin Howell, whose descendants sold the home and acreage to Multnomah County in 1961. Five years later, the Oregon Historical Society restored the estate to exactly the way it looked when Bybee carried his wife, Julia, over the threshold in 1856. Today, it's the centerpiece of Howell Territorial Park, a 120-acre nature preserve. It is a popular picnic destination for bicyclists, who descend en masse upon the bucolic island at the confluence of the Willamette and Columbia during the summer months.

The new Sauvie Island Bridge (foreground) is shown here being jacked into place over Multnomah Channel in late December 2007. Portland mayor Sam Adams (then a city councilor) proposed reusing the former span (background), which dates from 1950, as a pedestrian bridge over I-405 to link Northwest Portland's Pearl District and Nob Hill neighborhoods, but the moving bill would've cost more than a new bridge. The old Sauvie Island Bridge was sent to Schnitzer Steel, fed into a shredding machine, and recycled.

Albert Alonzo Durham

In this photograph, circa 1890, iron workers are dwarfed by the blast furnace (at 60 feet tall) at the Oregon & Steel Company's Pipe foundry in Oswego, which was modeled after a design by Andrew Carnegie. The plant produced iron for buildings in downtown Portland, as well as San Francisco's City Hall (which was destroyed in the earthquake of 1906). At its height in 1890, the foundry employed more than 300 people, including 150 Chinese laborers.

# LAKE OSWEGO

As Mary Goodall wrote in her 1958 history of Lake Oswego, *Oregon's Iron Dream*, entrepreneur Albert Alonzo Durham left Springfield, Illinois, in 1847 on the advice of his friend, an attorney named Abraham Lincoln. Durham took his wife and three young children on a wagon train to Oregon City, where he set up a sawmill on the banks of the Clackamas River at John McLoughlin's ambitious new townsite. Two years later, like many of the men in Oregon Country, Durham left on a steamer to find his fortune panning for gold along California's American River. But unlike most, Durham struck it rich. When he returned to Oregon City in 1850, he decided to found his own townsite. He packed up his family, floated downstream a couple of miles, and filed a donation land claim for 637 acres on the west bank of the Willamette at Sucker Creek, a stream

fed by a lake Native Americans called Waluga, for its proliferation of wild swans but referred to as Sucker Lake by locals for its plethora of *Catostomus*, or suckerfish. Durham built a sawmill powered by a 36-foot-high waterwheel, began selling lumber to Portlanders, and platted a town he called Oswego, named for his birthplace in upstate New York.

After iron ore was discovered in the hills above Sucker Lake, a group of investors from downtown Portland bought up land around the creek and lake and formed the Oregon Iron Company, vowing that Oswego would become "the Pittsburgh of the West." They built a smelter and smokestack—the first foundry west of the Mississippi. On August 24, 1867, they began producing pig iron and cast-iron pipe. Over the next

27 years, under various incarnations, the foundry churned out 166 million pounds of iron, much of it destined for buildings in Portland's business district. Due to higher-quality material from the East and falling prices, the blast furnace was extinguished in 1894. In 1910, The Ladd Estate Company, which held the title to the foundry's industrial lands, began transforming Oswego into Portland's most affluent suburb. Homes on Oswego Lake (the name was changed in 1913) routinely sell for more than a million dollars, and golfers at Oswego Lake Country Club off Iron Mountain Boulevard (founded in 1924 with the motto "Live Where You Play") are oblivious to the abandoned mine tunnels below the links. The Ladd Estate Company's 1920 real estate office on 10th Street is headquarters for the city's historical society, the Oswego Heritage Council.

Scaffolding obscures Oregon Iron Company's historic 1867 smelter, which is undergoing a federally funded historic restoration.

The cottage pictured here at 40 Wilbur Street in Old Town is one of the last surviving homes the Oregon Iron Company built for its employees in the 1880s.

## WILLAMETTE METEORITE

CLACKAMAS NATION ELDERS CALLED THE ROCK *Tomanowos* and believed it was a piece of moon that had fallen from the sky—a sacred object that had figured into tribal rituals for generations. In 1902, a Welsh miner named Ellis G. Hughes stumbled across the giant potato-shape, pock-marked mound of iron that was half-buried in the dirt near the intersection of Sweetbriar and Grapevine roads in present-day West Linn, hit it with a rock hammer (producing a gong) and knew immediately what it was. With a horse and wire rope and logs used as rollers, Hughes spent three months hauling the nearly 16-ton mound of solid iron to his farm, erected a shack over it, and began charging visitors to view what he claimed was the world's biggest meteorite.

Noticing a trail from Hughes's shack to a pit on property owned by Lake Oswego's Oregon Iron & Steel Company, the foundry claimed Hughes had stolen it, sued the prospector, and won. In 1905, the meteorite was floated down the Willamette to Guild's Lake and displayed at the Lewis and Clark Centennial Exposition. It attracted the attention of a collector from New York City who purchased the artifact for $20,600 and donated it to the American Museum of Natural History. Although the museum has declined repeated requests for repatriation of *Tomanowos* (shown below—it's the sixth largest meteorite in the world and the largest in the United States), it allows representatives from the Confederated Tribes of Grand Ronde to pay their respects once a year in the exhibition hall.

Water skiers Diane Spencer Nicholas, a veteran of Florida's Cypress Gardens, and her husband Don Nicholas perform at the Oswego Water Festival in 1958.

*Left:* Lake Oswego's main street, State Street, was still a dirt road when a photographer snapped this image of the Oswego Depot, circa 1910. The newly incorporated Oswego's makeover from industrial capital of the Northwest to Portland's classiest suburban enclave was just beginning.

*Via Regia,* a stainless steel abstract sculpture by Bay Area artist Stephen Fitz-Gerald sits on a pedestal at the corner of A Avenue and State Street. It is one of 58 sculptures installed on sidewalks throughout the city as part of the Arts Council of Lake Oswego's *Gallery Without Walls* ongoing outdoor exhibition.

One of Southern Pacific's Oregon Electric Railway (known as the "Red Electric" for the distinctive crimson paint job of its rolling stock) interurban commuter trains approaches the Oswego Depot in 1914. Daily service from Portland's Union Station to Corvallis began in 1912 and ended in 1929, jump-starting the city's emergence as a bedroom community.

The Oregon Electric Railway Historical Society's vintage Willamette Shore Trolley retraces the former Red Electric line's route along Southwest Portland's waterfront. The nonprofit has been operating excursion trains on the six-mile stretch between Lake Oswego's old depot and Portland's South Waterfront neighborhood since 1987. They're waiting for the day when the Portland Streetcar will restore commuter service between the two cities.

## Present Day Oswego Lake

Today, waterfront homes on bucolic Oswego Lake (known as Sucker Lake when the city was founded in the 1850s) routinely sell for well over $1 million. In early 2009, the 1930s-era estate of swimwear tycoon Carl Jantzen, a 13,000 square-foot Tudor mansion on a private 5.5-acre island, was on the market for $19.5 million. The sprawling development at the corner of State Street and A Avenue (bottom) is Lake View Village, a $22 million outdoor shopping mall that opened in November 2003.

# OREGON CITY

By the turn of the century, Portland had long since eclipsed Oregon City. After all, with a population of 90,000, in 1900, the Rose City was 26 times the size of the metropolis on the east bank of the Willamette Falls. But Oregon City, which promoted itself as the "Niagara of the Pacific," wasn't about to accept second-class status.

"Aside from her location at the falls of the Willamette, one of the greatest water-powers on the continent... Oregon City has other features of interest that attract attention and challenge admiration," wrote the *Oregon City Courier-Herald* in a commemorative edition published on New Year's Day 1901.

Those features included seven schoolhouses with 25 teachers, two banks and newspapers, four hotels, three livery stables, a $60,000 courthouse, and the first suspension bridge west of the Mississippi. But that was only one of many firsts: first city west of the Rockies, first land office in the west, first hotel in Oregon, first jail in Oregon, Oregon's first telegraph message (to Portland in 1855), first hydroelectric power plant west of the Mississippi, and the first long-distance transmission of electricity in the nation (in 1889 from Willamette Falls to power 55 streetlamps in Portland, 14 miles away).

A century later, the U.S. Census counted 30,667 people in Oregon City, far short of the 529,121 living in Portland. But at the Niagara of the Pacific, where the same hydroelectric generators still crackle and hum as they did at the dawn of the 20th century, Oregon City can't claim to be the most populous city on the Willamette. It could boast that it's the most powerful, if not for one thing: Portland General Electric's T. W. Sullivan Plant, which has been generating electricity since 1895, lies on the west side of the falls, within the boundaries of West Linn, another ascendant river city that was incorporated in 1913.

At the turn of the century when this photograph was taken, Oregon City's Willamette Falls, sometimes called the "Niagara of the Pacific," attracted sightseers and "hog lines" (boats strung together) of fisherman casting for salmon.

A modern-day hog line trolls for spring chinook at the foot of the falls, one of the most prolific fisheries in the Pacific Northwest.

In this image from the late 1880s, a steamboat transits the Willamette Falls Locks, which opened the Willamette River upstream from the falls to navigation on January 1, 1873. Willamette Falls Locks, now maintained by the Army Corps of Engineers, are the oldest continually operated multichambered locks in the United States.

On June 3, 1889, the Willamette Falls Electric Company's Station A hydropower plant (the two-story whitewashed structure on the ledge at the head of the falls, photographed here in 1894) became the first in the nation to send power down long-distance transmission lines.

The first Oregon City Bridge (pictured here in the 1890s), was designed to carry wagons and electricity. The first long-distance power transmission lines in the United States were strung over its twin towers.

Businesses along Oregon City's Main Street have struggled to survive competition from nearby superstores. In 2008, Oregon City was one of ten cities statewide selected to participate in the Oregon Main Street program, a statewide effort to revive historic downtown business districts.

A horse-drawn wagon clip-clops along Main Street in this circa 1910 photograph of downtown Oregon City. "During the year 1894 the main business street of Oregon City was paved with brick at a cost somewhat exceeding $40,000. This was the first brick pavement in the Northwest, and gives entire satisfaction," the *Oregon City Courier-Herald* reminded its readers in 1900. "Other streets have been extensively improved, making them handsome and modern thoroughfares."

Visitors ascend the steps of Oregon City's End of the Oregon Trail Interpretive Center, a museum commemorating Oregon City's history as the western terminus of the Barlow Road, the final leg of the storied Oregon Trail. In November 2003, one year after these photographs were taken, a windstorm shredded the iconic Conestoga-like bonnet shrouding the main entrance. Due to lack of funding, it was never replaced. On March 9, 2009, battered by the economic recession, the museum, which opened in 1995, closed its doors. However, thanks to new funding, the Oregon Trail Interpretive Center reopened two months later.

When Oregon City founder John McLoughlin built his home on Main Street in 1845, it was said to be the largest house in Oregon. It is pictured here on August 17, 1939, 30 years after it was relocated to a public park.

The paper mill shown in this February 1966 photograph dates from 1889, when Willamette Pulp & Paper first harnessed the power of the Willamette Falls. Now owned by West Linn Paper Company, the factory produces 700 tons of paper per day.

## OREGON CITY ELEVATOR

**WHEN OREGON CITY FOUNDER JOHN MCLOUGHLIN** built his house in 1846, the two-story colonial was the biggest in the state and stood in the heart of the city. But by the turn of the century, a proliferation of woolen mills, sawmills, and other factories had forced the residential district to move the only direction it could—up.

In 1909, the city used a mechanical winch to hoist the McLoughlin House 92 feet up the cliff to join other homes at the top of the bluff. Six years later, in deference to the arduous commute of bluff dwellers (via four stairways, with anywhere from 150 to 350 steps) who worked along the waterfront, the city built a municipal elevator, calling it the world's first vertical street. Like every appliance in Oregon City, the city's people-mover was powered by the river, with water pressure that pushed the lift skyward—to the chagrin of homeowners on the bluff, it also sucked water away from kitchen sinks and bathtubs with every load (up to 3,800 passengers a day). In 1955, the vintage wooden hydropowered structure—converted to electricity in 1924—was scrapped for the electric elevator that's used today.

Oregon City's electric municipal elevator is shown (at right) still under construction in 1955. It replaced the city's first elevator (at left), which, when it was built in 1915, whisked riders on a column of water.

# INDEX